THE ATLANTIC CRITICAL REVIEW

QUARTERLY

A Peer Reviewed Journal Indexed in
MLA Directory of Periodicals

OCTOBER – DECEMBER 2015

VOLUME 14 NUMBER 4

ATLANTIC

PUBLISHERS & DISTRIBUTORS (P) LTD

CONTRIBUTORS

Jeffery Moser. British Renaissance Scholar and Ph.D., A.B.D., University of Denver, USA.

Jalal Uddin Khan. Professor of English, University of Nizwa, Oman.

Anita Myles. Professor, Department of English, D.D.U. Gorakhpur University, Gorakhpur.

Shahaji V. Gaikwad. Associate Professor and Head, Department of English, M.S.S. Arts, Commerce and Science College Jalna.

Reena Mitra. Professor of English, Amity School of Languages, Amity University, Lucknow, Uttar Pradesh.

Binod Kumar Roy. Head, Department of English, R.S.S. College, Chochahan, BRABU.

Amit Kumar. Assistant Teacher, Bhagwanpur High School, Samastipur.

Shivani Mallick. Research Scholar, LNMU Darbhanga.

Priyankar Dutta. Assistant Teacher, Chandrapur Junior High School, Birbhum, West Bengal.

Anju Bala Agrawal. Associate Professor, Department of English, R.C.A. Girls College, Mathura.

Sunanda Mishra. Reader in English, K.K.S. Women's College Balasore, Odisha.

THE ATLANTIC CRITICAL REVIEW
VOLUME 14 NUMBER 4 (OCTOBER-DECEMBER 2015)

CONTENTS

Tudor Peril, Protestant Doctrine, and the Poetical in Parr's Prayers

JEFFERY MOSER

THIS study is about Katherine Parr's early modern devotional writings. Parr (Aug. 1512-5 Sep. 1548) was the sixth and last wife of King Henry Tudor VIII, and served as a tutor, lecturer, and scholar in the Tudor Court. Her writings are worthy study because of their literary merit and the cultural lens into creativities and strategies pursued by Parr and other women during the literary, political, and cultural complexities of the Renaissance in England.

Once married to King Henry VIII, Katherine Parr had direct access to the Royal Library which included books collected by the king and other members of the Tudor Family dynasty. She would have perused this vast collection of pamphlets, manuscripts, and books of classical antecedent and English vernacular, along with works by continental authors. Further, as Henry's wife, Parr was the intimate eyes and ears to one of the most intelligent and widely read monarchs of the renaissance who was well-versed and involved in theological debate and monastic history, especially when he broke England away from Rome (Carley 1-20).

At the same time, Henry VIII was a humanist scholar and head of his time in all of the liberal arts, especially music and poetry. Equally, most of his wives were also avid readers and collected a variety of books. Hence, Katherine would have been able to access and read some works held in Henry's collection that were accumulated by the women who preceded her as his wife. She would have read the marginalia in these women's hands plus the marginalia in books in Henry's own hand. These added to Parr's knowledge about the politics of class, gender, religion, and literary production. As she read and wrote, there is no question that Parr developed a keen sense about women's subjectivity within male-authored texts and religious doctrine, as well as through her own experiences of class rise and unexpected elevation to royalty.

Parr was a wealthy widow when she married for the third time and became queen consort of England and Ireland in 1543. As Henry VIII's sixth wife, she became "lover" to an aging and increasingly rotund and ailing king (Henry VIII reigned from 21 Apr. 1509 to 28 Jan. 1547). While she was the only spouse of Henry's to outlive him, this accomplishment was due more to a matter of defying fate or even providence than from Parr's constancy in loving and loyal matrimonial servitude and gender subservience. She bore Henry's tirades and quick temper with undeserved patience and humility, and so it was that Parr managed to not become one of his court victims.

After Henry died in January of 1547, Parr lived another twenty months, eventually succumbing to complications during pregnancy. She bore a daughter named Mary, her only child. The infant's father was Thomas Seymour, 1st Baron of Sudeley (c. 1508-20 Mar. 1549), and he came from a family that had been intimately entwined with the Tudor royals and their courts. When Parr married this fourth husband, the two had already known one another for a long time. They had been sweethearts many years before Parr was chosen by Henry to be his wife, and even before she joined the Tudor court as a member of the household for the king's eldest daughter, Mary; this particular alliance stemmed from Katherine's late mother's former friendship with the former queen and Henry's first wife, Catherine of Aragon, Henry's first wife. Katherine returned the favor by naming her only child after Aragon's daughter.

Specifically related to literature, Parr produced two significant writings which were published and printed as bound books. *The Lamentation of a Sinner* was written in the winter of 1545-46 and published in November of 1547. *Lamentation* was preceded by a smaller, earlier devotional work titled, *Prayers or Meditations: Wherein the Mind is Stirred Patiently to Suffer All Afflictions* (pub. 6 Nov. 1545). They complete a pair of shared religious writings and personal meditations that challenge prevailing ideals about the patriarchal dominance of early English literature (Carley 138). From a literary standpoint, the two works, while slim, are phenomenal, considering that each was published during Parr's own lifetime, while Henry, too, was alive, and when poetry was the favored genre of the Tudor Age. Her writing stands alone in the privileged public craft of poetry, a writing enterprise and court pastime that was largely reserved for and aspired to by men of societal stature.

Prayers or Meditations is the more poetical of the two literary works. It is more personal than Parr's second assembled devotions and elucidates significant views about biblical exegesis, church doctrine, and gender expectations. Five original prayers are appended to *Prayers or Meditations* and they serve as a fitting close to this initial volume. The five prayers are titled as follows: (1) "A prayer for the king," (2) "A prayer for men to say entering into battle," (3) "A devout prayer to be daily said" (this is the longest of the five prayers), (4) "An other prayer," (this is the shortest prayer at 27 lines), and finally (5) "A devout prayer" (almost as brief as the fourth prayer).

Indeed, while the surface, style, and structure of Parr's prayers are undeniably prose, each prayer reflects common qualities in middle- to late-sixteenth century English Renaissance writings that were set to music and poetry. Hence, Parr's prayers should be viewed as prose poetry. Not only does the arrangement of Parr's prayers reveal her bookish background and educated scholarship, but characteristics of poetic rhythm, calculated word choice, and regulated number of syllables are exhibited. Additionally, Parr employs an inventive use of the translated and transformed Petrarchan conceit, and she expresses very personal desires and passion, common to poems in her day.

Overall, Parr's prayers resemble meter and line found in sonnets and songs that were widely written and circulated by poets enamored in the male enterprise of early Tudor court poetry. These poems influenced late-sixteenth century poets like Sidney, Spenser, and Shakespeare. Parr's prose prayers embody lyricism and power, not unlike Sir Edmund Spenser who pledged "loving service to the royal mistress" (Malcolmson 88). However, Parr's prayers focus on the English monarchy and compare her husband and royal family to the Family of God. As Elizabeth I would later show, Parr takes advantage of her femininity and class status to delineate and dictate female literary prowess and control over history as she shores up the superiority of the English church-state ordered by male power. For example, in "A prayer for the king," Parr pays homage to her God and her husband's majesty. She acknowledges the divine power that is bestowed upon English monarchy, and her prayer-poem is about Henry's only living son, Prince Edward. Hence, carried in the poem's title and throughout are "king" and "kings" with lowercase "k." The typography may seem slight detail, but in print, this permitted Parr to equalize gender, suspend and sustain lyrical and power equations.

Accordingly, "A prayer for the king" begins just like authors or imitators invoke the Muses when writing a hymn or poetry: "O LORD,

Jesus Christ, most high, most mighty,/ king of kings, lord of lords, the only tu-/ late of princes, the very son of God/ on whose right hand sitting." Parr continues by replicating the traditional patterns in epic poetry. She sets down more history and imparts an ability meant to excite the poet's creativity and passion and call forth the Muses. In this case, she is calling forth God's creative spirit so that the future king shall also create, i.e. rule. Further, Parr asks that Henry's only son Edward be guided and protected in order "to replenish him with the/ grace of the holy spirit, that he always(s)/ incline to thy will, and walk in thy way."

On another level, Parr's prayer suggests that she, too, is asking for God to grant her with the ability to be inspired, to create, and write. By asking for God's help, the poet reveals that she, herself (and even her readers) is (are) no less devoted to Him. It is therefore to be understood that she (they/we as readers) recognize herself/(ourselves) as a sinner(s). She (they/we) confess her(our) sins, and therefore, only by God's grace, Parr and "we", as readers, are worthy hence to be held in favor and protected from harm: "With most lowly hearts we beseech thee, vouch-/ safe, with favorable regard, to behold/ our most gracious sovereign lord, king Edward/ the VI, and to replenish him with the grace of the holy spirit, that he always/ incline to thy will, and walk in thy way." On its surface, this very lyrical prose prayer resembles any ordinary devotion. The tone is soft, the mood is devout, and the poet presents herself lowly and humbly before her omnipotent, omniscient, and omnipresent God. However, the composer is an extraordinary lady, queen, and woman deeply committed to Christian ideals, morality, and theological scholarship.

Also, similar to the opening of a hymn or epic poem, this prayer, as well as each of Parr's other four prayers, call out the poet's desires for the protection, instruction, health, wealth, glory, honor, joy of countenance, and strength for the not-yet-of-age Edward, son of the presiding "king". At one level, Parr's requests are figments of the "praying poet's" imagination and they do not exist. Also, they are heartfelt expressions by a stepmother. On another level, everything cited is very real, vital to the poet who writes, and thus stands for every believer's creative endeavor. Without prayerful desires, Parr's "we" (readers and Protestant Christian believers) would be robbed of our own creative power and purpose. Therefore, concerns within this poem function as images and details of social history, and hence, the poem projects these images and details as possibilities and specifics. The overall message is pertinent: England is God's kingdom on Earth and Tudor King Henry VIII and his son Edward reign as the human presence of God, the Father and his son, the Lord Jesus Christ. Thus, the poet Parr acts as their disciple and her prayer-poem animates the Holy Ghost in order to complete the triune God of all creation—natural and artistic—and God's grace.

Still, wholly on another level, Parr exhibits theological acumen and literary genius by supplanting social context. Safety for herself and every English person is requested within "A prayer for the king." Her purpose is the idealization of salvation, made possible through the Tudor Dynasty and which shall be sustained through Edward and his anticipated socio-political future. While the poem is historically and theologically centered, Parr employs metaphor. This makes her prayer a mirror of the Lord's Prayer articulated in Holy Scripture in Matthew 6:9-15. In Parr's time, the Lord's Prayer was central to Holy Communion, and it was also a part of the structured liturgy in worship for both the Roman Catholic and early Anglican churches. Eventually, the Lord's Prayer was set down in the first Protestant *Book of Common Prayer*, published in 1549 and during the reign of Edward VI, exactly as Parr envisioned.

The Book of Common Prayer was the product of the English Reformation and reflected significant religious development of Christianity on the British Isles. Here is how the Lord's Prayer appears in *The Book of Common Prayer* of 1549, published and distributed throughout England a few months after Parr died in late-1548:

> Let us praye. (Stated by the priest)
>
> As our saviour Christe hath commaunded and taught us, we are bolde to saye. Our father, whyche art in heaven, halowed be thy name. Thy Kyngdome come. Thy wyll be doen in yearth, as it is in heaven. Geve us this daye our dayly breade. And forgeve us our trespaces, as wee forgeve them that trespasse agaynst us. And leade us not into temptacion. The aunswere. (Congregation answers) But deliver us from evill. Amen.

Hence, there are multiple contexts and concerns within Parr's prayer. Not only is her lyrical devotion a suspended prayer for the lords of the court but also a sustained instrument of the contemplative Lord's Prayer and a reflection of reformed Protestant belief. For early Tudor court poets and devotional writers in the sixteenth century, their works also carry vital images and secular and religious messages. Court poetry allowed poets to entertain, inform and educate readers about writing, the poets themselves, the court, and destiny of their nation and souls, and all, if the poets were wary and wise, with discretion and from the distance writing permitted.

Likewise, Parr's prayers produce an effect that is compressed and paradoxical, requiring imagination and intellect on the part of her readers to unravel the analogies. They resemble the parables that Jesus told and which are detailed in the Gospels. Without doubt, Parr understood metaphor and the poetic conceit, which Sir Thomas Wyatt, Henry Howard, the earl of Surrey, and other English writers translated from Italian and transformed into English poetry. Poignantly, Parr was England's first queen to have creative works publicly appear in print, the first queen to publish a book under her own name, and the first early modern Englishwoman to be published after the year 1500, although it is highly unlikely she would have ever considered herself an "author" or "published" as these terms and other ideals, including that of modern copyright were not yet firmly established.

Again, this notion of secular religious authorship and creative work, i.e. original poetry, were first and almost exclusively ascribed to male writers in the sixteenth century. Nonetheless, Parr would have read and listened to love sonnets and scriptural verse such as those from the Psalter and which early Tudor court poets translated. Scholar Kimberly Coles has noted that there was virtually no imitation of lyric translations of the Psalms, nor what could be termed secular songs and sonnets, not even closely tied to even a Christian passion, written by early modern women between 1549 and 1591 (15), and thus none before them either. Therefore, in spite of Parr writing in prose and not crafting poetry, her devotional prayers show ingenuity nevertheless and impart recognizable patterns of poetry and poetics.

Assuredly, Parr would have met priests and poets and seen their writings firsthand as they came to court and circulated their manuscripts, even when these works were read out loud and/or sung as instruction or entertainment for the king, Parr, and his court. So, too, would Henry's five previous wives have read and observed these writings, as well as other ladies at court, i.e. ladies in waiting who served the sorted queens and in various ranks as Ladies of the Bedchamber, Ladies of the Privy Chamber, maids of honor and other women who assisted them. Most of these women, too, would have been privy to the court poets and their poems when they presented a copies to Henry. Poets shared early sonnets and other verse poems to the king and queen whose court and attention served as supreme audience. By Parr's nature, she would have been a most pleasantly kind and attentive audience to the poets and their performances (Felch 3-4).

Less than a decade after Parr died, England's first poetic anthology, *Songs and Sonnets*, also known as "*Tottel's Miscellany*" was printed in London and widely distributed, eventually proffering eight different printings. An extensive collection containing 310 poems, the *Miscellany* included sonnets (most translations of Italian renaissance poetry), ballads, and other poems in the English vernacular. These poems were ascribed most prominently to Henry Howard, the earl of Surrey, and Sir Thomas Wyatt, Henry's two diplomatic court advisers. This anthology also contained additional poems by Nicholas Grimald, under-editor to publisher Richard Tottel, plus poems by other poets that were labeled as "Uncertain auctyours" ("Uncertain authors") on the publication's title page. Wyatt and Surrey's first Petrarchan sonnet translations were composed sporadically between 1528 and 1547 (Foley xiii-xv), hence poems written and circulated while Parr was at court, perhaps as early as 1534, since, at the age of 22, Katherine secondly married John Neville, 3rd Baron of Latimer, and thus, she became a member of the peerage. Many of the poems collected in the *Miscellany* laid the groundwork for early modern poetics and authorship. In 1589, George Puttenham pronounced of Wyatt and Surrey that they:

> ...were the two chieftains, who having traveled into Italy, and there tasted the sweet and stately measures and style of Italian Poesie as novices newly crept out of the schools of Dante Arisote and Petrarch, from that it had been before, and for that cause may be justly be said the first reformers of our English meter and style. (34)

Parr would have been among the first female eyes and ears to these court poets' manuscript creations which harbored poetry reconfigured from the best poetry written on the continent and building on English tradition that had been set down by medieval monks, Chaucer and the Ricardian poets, and other late-medieval and early modern English and Scottish poets. Hence, Parr must be considered one of the first female critics of poetry, and, unbeknown to the renaissance court poets, a pre-formal "protégé" of their refined poetic meters and forms in English vernacular.

However, again, while translation and poetry were in vogue, printing remained a developing industry during Parr's lifetime. Creative authorship and the production of original verse poetry were enterprises largely delegated to men. Also, book selling and buying were transacted by men. Yet, together with being the premier audience for court poets and with concern for her own survival as Henry's wife and queen, Parr should be remembered for her steadfastness after converting to Protestantism, her boldness as an early Protestant reformer, and one of the first authors of Protestant devotional writing. Essentially, devotional writing was the one and only venue of literary enterprise and semi-social activity reserved for women. The genre was largely abandoned or dismissed by male writers of the Age.

Perhaps more accurately, the genre of devotions was virtually ignored by Englishmen seeking prestige and power. Other than devotional writing, avenues of secular or sacred communications such as speeches, poems, academic lessons, sermons, public prayers, etc.,—all forms of rhetorical, reputable, popular, and socially acceptable texts with public consequence during the middle of the sixteenth century—were subsumed of, controlled by, and exclusively reserved for the prevue of men in Tudor society. Nonetheless, early modern wives and daughters had access to the books of men in their homes, and as humanist grammar schools developed for boys, girls were taught to read at home and church. Hence, devotional writing and religious teachings, while very much a private and homosocial exercise for women, offered females a lucrative path and creative venue for reading and writing. Certainly, devotions were advocated and appreciated by the Protestant reformers of the male-centered English church-state. Because devotions instilled temperance, patience, and courage for their dedicatees, path setters like Parr and other women inside and outside of the court helped to spread their teaching and thus, helped to encourage and spread literacy. While Parr prayed, she transcribed and shared her spoken and written devotions with women around her. As printing advanced, especially after 1550, more women followed Parr's bi-partite private and public authorial path, including, and of course, with Henry VIII's two daughters and her step-daughters, Mary and Elizabeth Tudor, each of whom became queen regents and authors in their own time.

After Parr, more women translated and transcribed sacred and secular prose and poetry, composed original verse, and in the special cases of Mary and Elizabeth, wrote and gave prominent speeches in their respective roles as head of state. Poetically speaking, the verse exchanges between Elizabeth and Sir Walter Raleigh are well known and considered quality poems. But Parr also delivered official speeches and most likely played a role in the writing of them. Janel Mueller, scholar of early modern

Englishwomen and their essential works, has verified that, when Henry went on a military campaign in France in 1544, Katherine acted as appointed regent in his absence from July to September (x). According to Henry's orders set in writing, Katherine was to rule as Regent until Prince Edward came of age. During this time, documents carrying Katherine's signature ("Kateryn the Quene, K.P." or "Kateryne the Quene Regente, K.P.") multiplied and attested a self-cognizant identity in her stable notion of how to spell her name and her remarkable insistence on preserving a trace of her birth name by appended initials (Mueller x). Obviously, the idea of feminine authorship was underway and Parr validated the role for other Englishwomen as she served as their queen and acting head of state on the home front.

Further, by 1545-46, Katherine Parr gained notoriety through her reading and discussing scripture with a circle of ladies in her chamber (Mueller x). Parr and other women were at the forefront of the Henrician Court in defending the emerging Protestant religion (Felch 8). Of note, Parr's circle of female reformers included another eventual published author of devotional writings: Elizabeth Tyrwhit. Tyrwhit was well established at court, along with her husband Robert who served as the king's master of the horse. Tyrwhit first served as Lady of the Privy Chamber to Jane Seymour, Prince Edward's mother. Later, she became Lady of the Privy Chamber for Katherine. It was Tyrwhit who set down in writing and reported Katherine's dowager to the court upon her death.

Finally, it is well documented how Katherine occasionally challenged Henry about theology, leaving the converted Protestant queen open to machinations by the conservative court faction that were well aware of Katherine's previous one-time and more-pronounced Catholic affiliations. Her arguments and external scheming mortally endangered Parr, leading to a staged confrontation before Henry by the enmity of powerful Catholic officials seeking to turn the king against his newly converted Protestant wife.

Upon Henry's return, the very educated, well-mannered, and quick-witted Katherine timed and averted a signed warrant for her arrest, and she and the king were soon reconciled. The queen offered submissive explanation that deferred to her husband's superior wisdom, telling Henry that "women by their first creation were made subject to men." She stated that men were "out to instruct wives, who would do all their learning from them." Further, Parr assured Henry that he was a "prince of such excellent learning and wisdom that" she would "gladly follow his counsel," for she had only taken the freedom to argue with him to "learn from him and distract him from his illness" (Starkey 600). Poetic justice or not, this brush with treason and execution saved Parr's credit with her husband and her life. However, this model of servitude did not save that of one of her other Protestant reformers. Writer and friend Anne Askew went to the stake in July 1546 (Mueller xi).

Katherine Parr even went onto reconcile Henry with his two daughters. She tutored Elizabeth in her education and learning and earlier encouraged Elizabeth's sister, Mary, her elder by 16 years, to translate Italian poetry and other continental prose. Thus, is it any surprise Katherine Parr's first original prayer in *Prayers or Meditations* is "A prayer for the king"? Foremost is that Parr was devoted to her husband and king, her Protestant God, and her position within these kingdoms. She publicly declared her motto on her wedding day, "To be useful in all I do" (British History Online, n.p.). Thereafter, Parr knew her allegiance was to God and king and these were the two lords defining her position and purpose as helpmate and first subject to Henry whom long before declared himself head of church and state. Thus, as already noted, her first original prayer, the second shortest of the five, is laced with expressions of love, loyalty and poetic alliteration. While structured as prose and no seeming poetic lines or stanzas in her prayers as they were first printed in black calligraphy font, they do however resemble songs.

"A prayer for the king" is not a direct address to Henry but about his son and eventual successor, Edward. This prayer is an urgent plea and concern for the prince's health and success as much as the prayer is poetry, with movement and an artful turn toward hope for the poet and her future as dowager queen. The prayer embodies passion. The poet expresses her heartfelt concern for her own security and provision upon her eventual removal from the court at some later date with her husband's passing, all of which came true. Below, is the full text of Parr's prose prayer but revised from its first printing. I crafted it into three stanzas and retained Parr's punctuation with the colon as signifier of her unifying or stanzaic thought(s). Also, I set her lines as best as possible to iambic pentameter without changing any of the original words or syllables, other than modernizing the spelling:

A prayer for the king

O LORD Jesus Christ, most high, most mighty,
king of kings, lord of lords, the only tu-

late of princes, the very son of God,
on whose right hand sitting, dost from thy throne
behold all the dwellers upon earth:

[W]ith most lowly hearts we beseech thee, vouch-
safe, with favorable regard, to behold
our most gracious sovereign lord, king Edward
the VI, and to replenish him with the
grace of the holy spirit, that he always[s]
incline to thy will, and walk in thy way.
Keep him far from ignorance, but through thy
gift let prudence and knowledge always[s] abound
in his total heart:

So instruct him (O LORD JESUS) reigning
upon us in earth, that his human majesty
sty, always obey thy divine majesty in
fear and dread. Imbue him plentifully
with heavenly gifts. Grant him in health and
wealth long to live. Heap glory and honor
upon him. Glad him with joy of thy counenance.
So strength him, that he may vanquish
and overcome all his and our foes, and he
be dread and feared of all the enemies of his realm. (Amen)

This illustrates more clearly the poetic nature of the prayer and its rich semblance to poetic meter and form. The number of syllables and punctuation chosen by Parr show familiarity with the emerging iambic stress metrical pattern (unstressed + stressed) that dominated English poetry of her time. Further, with slight editing to the familiar style of court-verse in rhyme or blank verse (the latter introduced by Surrey and perfected by Shakespeare), then visualized is these poetics of Parr's writing. Consider her two phrases, one in pentameter and one in the familiar early modern Poulter's measure (line with fourteen feet): "Grant him / in health / and wealth / [for] long / to live", or "and he / be dread / and feared / of all / the en'/ mies of / his realm", etc. With modest editing of syllables, caesuras, and a few line breaks this and all of Parr's prose prayers can be re-arranged and fashioned into readily-recognized poetic verse.

After Parr's devotions were printed, they were immediately distributed to her court ladies in the fashion poems by men were circulated. Largely,

Parr's other devotions in Prayers are reworked renditions of Thomas a' Kempis' Imitation of Christ, but her five closing prayers indicate her inspiration and intentions were, as Janel Mueller determined in 1996, to offer an English vernacular manual for private devotion and recitation yet for enjoyment and remembrance, too, like poetry was intended. The prayers were meant to be read and recited privately and often, i.e. more than once daily, and ultimately, memorized. These were the very same expectations and affectations for renaissance music and poems. Hence, Parr's construction of her prayers, with their brevity and quasi-poetics, reveal her logical craft and ingenious thought that she put into them. They gave readers pieces to easily recall and recite in the same vogue that English poetry was being performed, read privately, and memorized from print.

"An other prayer," Parr's shortest, exhibits common characteristics of poetry, too. The recitation and memorization of this short prayer are easy. As first published, this prayer-poem is 27 lines. That nearly equals two English sonnets of 14 lines a piece. Also, the prayer's content adheres to regular syllabic or 10-foot count in a single sonnet, either as the preferred iambic pentameter that Wyatt structured his sonnets or with the rhyme patterns of blank verse which Surrey initiated. Their poetic forms were on the rise during Parr's time, and she well knew the Petrarchan sonnet form from which Wyatt and Surrey modeled their sonnets of complaint, will and desire. Here follows Parr's poem:

An other prayer

O HEAVENLY FATHER,
God almighty, I pray and
beseech thy mercy, benignly to
behold me thy unworthy servant,
that I may by gift of
thy holy spirit, fervently desire
thy kingdom, that I may
know thy will, and work thereafter
after. Give me (O Lord) wisdom:

Make me constant, patient
and strong in thee. Keep
me lord, from the slighty innuation
of the old wily serpent.

Defend me from the counsels
and cursings of evil tongues.
Let thy mighty army be
my shield against all thy malignity
of this wicked world.
remember not (lord) mine offenses:
instruct, prepare me to
repent, to be sorry for my sins:

Make me to love Justice and
hate wrong, to do good, and
abstain from all evils: that I
may be worthy, to be called thy
child. To thee be honor and
glory for ever and ever. Amen.

Interesting, aside from the fact that this prose prayer, like its other four accompanying prayers was printed in long-hand calligraphy, there is nevertheless a displayed preference for the familiar five-foot meter of court poetry that was Anglicized and promoted by the poets who served Tudor King Henry VIII as his diplomats, advisers, and attendants. Just as poetical, where the astute queen crafted, "Let thy migh / ty ar / my be / my shield // against / all thy / ma lig / nity of / this wick / ed world," a fairly consistent iambic (unstressed + stressed) stress pattern scans and most of Parr's meter is di- or tri-syllabic.

Still another example of this above effect exists in Parr's "A Devout Prayer". Here, the astute queen wrote, "Lord, hear / ken to / my words, / consi / der the thought / of mine heart, // Behold / how loud / I cry / unto thee. // Let my / just prayer / en ter / into / thine ears; / which un / feigned / ly com / eth from / mine heart." Either as the spondaic (stressed + stressed) or the iambic (unstressed + stressed) stress pattern, both metrical emphases are observed in the last four syllables of "Lord, hear/ ken to / my words", and as well with, "Behold / how loud / I cry / unto thee", the last three-syllable count of "unto thee" being amphibrachic (unstressed + stressed + unstressed) stress pattern. Hence, subverted within Parr's "prayerful prose" is real poetry and poetry reflecting very visible and audible metrical patterns. Her phrases possess lines that hardly violate patterns of poetic meter and form but rather, these are enforced by Parr's artful phrasing and word choices. Thus, while Katherine Parr's devotional works on first glance do not readily appear to resound with meter and syllabic verse structure, on more careful study, the devotions reflect artistic intelligence about poetics and the court's taste for poetry that modulated between exhibits of elaborate, intricate and perfectly regular designs and looser, syntactically-flexible styles of meter and form interspersed with plain language, subtle indirection, and conceit, and even conceit and metaphor of a Christian demur.

Again, in *Prayers or Meditations*, Parr's second to the last prayer in her series of five displays a very fervent personal wish: "Make me constant, patient, and strong in thee. Keep me lord, from the slighty innuation[s] of the old wily serpent; defend me from the counsels and cursings of evil tongues." Like the ninth line of a sonnet, Parr includes a turn in this prayer, too, and it is onto the subject of Satan. This narrative turn reflects changes in subject, movement, and message, just like Italian sonnets take. Only, a literary astute and court majesty like Katherine Parr, while also appearing and behaving as kind and humble wrote like she chose wisely and carefully, subtle and in subordination in order to appease her husband yet also to advance the cause of religious reform and writing, with perils constant and circling in Henry VIII's late and violent court. She penned valued and "vouchsafe" lines that were also versified. Parr's prayers exhibit the poetry of passion, patience, and self-fashioning which were fundamental to surviving the dangers of the Henrician court. A lot like the male poets of her time, Parr follows characteristic twists and turns of Tudor thought and perception in her own writing: "...we most humbly beseech thee, O Lord God of hosts, to turn the hearts of our enemies to the desire of peace, that no Christian blood be spilt, or else grant, O Lord, that with small effusion of blood, and to the little hurt and damage of innocents, we may to thy glory obtain victory" (from "A prayer for men" in *Prayers*). If this effect is somewhat non-systematic and confusing, Parr's work nonetheless shows her independence and fascination with order and self-fashion.

Parr's uniqueness, expressed in sixteenth-century verse and writing shows a firm understanding of poetic voice and craft. As the British Isles' first published woman author, there is little doubt Parr intended for her works to be read and shared. While she was very devout, she was also persistent and literary. Her translations and arranged verses of lament, moral exhortation, devotion, and prayer function similar to forms that enabled Renaissance poets to draw out particular responses from their readers. Renaissance poetry has a transcendent effect. In order to capture her own longings and wishes as an early modern woman, Parr pursued the genre of devotions to have her thoughts and art received by others, read, and preserved. With a kind of poetic justice, this was most accomplished with Prayers which went through double-digit editions, 17 in fact to 1640. Between 1545 and 1546 about 12,000 copies of Parr's collection were printed and distributed in the first six months alone (Carley 138-42). Who except Katherine Parr imagined that devotions as literature could have such masculine force through feminine appeal?

WORKS CITED

Carley, James P. *The Books of King Henry VIII and His Wives*. Preface David Starkey. London: The British Library, 2004. Print.

Coles, Kimberly Anne. *Religion, Reform, and Women's Writing in Early Modern England.* Cambridge, Eng.: Cambridge University Press, 2008. Print.

———. "Katherine Parr." Tudor Monarchs. *English History*. 3 May 2012. Web. 30 Oct. 2015.

Felch, Susan M. *Elizabeth Tyrwhit's Morning and Evening Prayers*. Aldershot: Ashgate, 2008. Print.

Foley, Stephen Merriam. *Sir Thomas Wyatt*. Boston, MA: Twayne-G.K. Hall, 1990. Print.

Hanson, Marilee. "Tudor Monarchs & Dynasty—Last English Tudor Monarchs History." HYPERLINK "http://englishhistory.net/tudor/tudor-monarchs/" http://englishhistory.net/tudor/tudor-monarchs/. 8. Feb. 2015. Web. 4 Nov. 2015.

Malcolmson, Cristina, ed. Renaissance Poetry. Intro. Cristina Malcolmson. London: Longman, 1998. Print.

Mueller, Janel, ed. *Printed Writings, 1500-1640: Katherine Parr*. Vol. 3. Gen. Eds. Betty S. Travitsky and Patrick Cullen. Intro. Janel Mueller. Aldershot: Scolar Press, 1996. Print.

Puttenham, George. *The Arte of English Poesie*. Eds. Gladys Doidge Willcock and Alice Walker. Cambridge, Eng.: Cambridge University Press, 1926. Print.

Starkey, David. *Six Wives: The Queens of Henry VIII*. New York: HarperCollins, 2004. Print.

The Book of Common Prayer. 1549. HYPERLINK "http://justus.anglican.org/resources/bcp/1549/Communion_1549.htm" \t "_blank" http://justus.anglican.org/resources/bcp/1549/Communion_1549.htm. Web author Charles.

Wohlers. 25 June 2015. Web. 15 Nov. 2015.

Literature of the New Year: Literary Variations on the Celebration of the New Year

JALAL UDDIN KHAN

THERE are many New Years throughout the world: Western January 1st; Celtic Samhain, meaning "Summer's End" on the eve of 31 October;[1] Arabic Muharram 1st (which being lunar based comes ahead by a week or so every year on the solar-based Western calendar); Jewish Rosh Hashanah, meaning "head of the year," that is, the first day of the month of Tishri on the Jewish calendar;[2] Iranian/Persian Nowruz, which means the New Day (first day of spring) and which roughly coincides with March 21st; Chinese New Year, also known as the Spring Festival, that falls between 21 January and 20 February, and the Bengali New Year or *Pohela Boishakh*, which according to the Indian solar calendar falls on 14 April.

All these dates were affected by Pope Gregory XIII when he corrected the errors of the Julian calendar, named after Julius Caesar. The latter gave a few minutes extra to the year. This extra time kept accumulating so that by the 16th century there was a difference of 10 days between the New Year and the natural or seasonal cycle of the year. With the help of the astronomers' calculation, Gregory ordered, in 1582, that throughout the Catholic world the 4th October would be followed by the 15th October. Protestant England, having led the opposition to Roman Catholicism, was hesitant for about two hundred years and then accepted the Gregorian calendar in 1752. However, England then cut another 11 days in September to bring the New Year and the season in accord. Thus, 21 days had to be retrenched, giving the impression of doubt or arbitrariness about the exact beginning of the New Year as mentioned above and below (by George William Curtis in his essay).

Let us, however, proceed by taking the widely celebrated January 1st for granted as the conventional beginning of the New Year that globally shapes and formats the life and affairs of the humankind worldwide.

There are countless poems and essays written in bidding farewell to the old year and welcoming the new.[3] If the anonymous medieval classic *Sir Gawain and the Green Knight* is an example, Christmas and the New Year do not just mean feasting, drinking and welcoming the new as routine but also meeting the weird, marvelous, supernatural and dangerous challenges, of course, in a noble and chivalrous manner. By contrast, seventeenth-century English poet Robert Herrick sends as his New Year's gift to an aristocrat (in his poem "A New Year's Gift, sent to Sir Simeon Steward") not a big news of national importance, good or bad, but a reminder of the simple local sports and the homely joys of meat, wine, and "plenteous harvest" that a common man in a small town or the countryside can enjoy with his family and friends during a peaceful year. Details of Herrick's New Year's gift include "a jolly"

Verse crown'd with ivy and with holly;
That tells of winter's tales and mirth
That milk-maids make about the hearth;
Of Christmas sports, the wassail-bowl,
That toss'd up, after Fox-i'-th'-hole;
Of Blind-man-buff, and of the care
That young men have to show the Mare;
Of twelfth-tide cakes, of peas and beans,
Wherewith ye make those merry scenes,
When as ye choose your king and queen,
And cry out, 'Hey for our town green!'

On a very generalized note, Herrick's younger contemporary Charles Cotton tells us about the New Year's fear of "direst mischiefs" as well as its "superexcellently good" fortunes through the appearance of the two-faced Janus, the ancient Roman God of beginnings and transitions, from whose name the month of January is traditionally thought to derive. Cotton, a "hearty and cheerful" man, as Charles Lamb calls him in his New Year's Eve essay (see below), ends his poem "The New Year" with a note of hope and optimism saying one good year in three is enough to welcome a new year and be happy.

What Herrick does not want on his New Year's gift list is the news of the momentous political events of the time. He does not mention what they are but they could probably be the defeat of the Spanish Armada and the Gun Powder Plot. These may very well be some of what Cotton refers to as the "direst mischiefs" or "superexcellently good" fortunes, national or individual. Herrick begins with what would be out of his list:

No news of navies burnt at seas;
No noise of late spawned tittyries;
No closet plot or open vent,
That frights men with a Parliament:
No new device or late-found trick,
To read by the stars the kingdom's sick;
No gin to catch the State, or wring
The free-born nostril of the King,
We send to you....

Centuries ago Britain's poet laureate introduced the tradition of writing a New Year poem. Laureate Nahum Tate established this practice, having written many New Year odes during his laureateship lasting for 23 years, starting from 1693, and being successively confirmed by three monarchs. Apart from the obligatory New Year and Birthday Odes and poems on the death of Queen Mary and Queen Anne, Tate in his laureate position wrote poems on the English victories by sea and land.[4]

It is exactly the similar national and international affairs moving and shaking the world at the time of the French Revolution that are referred to in *Ode to the Departing Year* (1796) by Samuel Taylor Coleridge. It is to be noted that Coleridge's Ode is on/to the departing year (not on the New Year), when he had still been in favour of France, before he turned against France for its aggression against other countries and its threat of invasion against England looming large. Together with the patriotic *Fears in Solitude*, the immediately following *France: An Ode* (April 1798) is in fact a recantation or palinodia as Coleridge called it expressing the withdrawal of his support from France. In *Ode to the Departing Year*, Coleridge focuses on the political developments, especially the death of Catherine of Russia, that were internationally disconcerting. Detesting his own England with pain and anguish, he makes a prophesy that Britain would fall if it entered an alliance with the tyrant Russia against what he then thought was still a promising revolutionary France. As in Herrick's poem, Coleridge's Ode ends with a recommendation for a simple life of hard work as a farmer in an agrarian setting close to soil—a recommendation that Coleridge was planning to translate into action as he was moving from Bristol to Nether Stowey, Somerset, in South West England with the intention of becoming a farmer himself.

Coleridge's *Ode to the Departing Year* is quoted from by his friend Charles Lamb in his essay "New Year's Eve," published in the January 1821 issue of *The London Magazine*. Author of *Tales from Shakespeare* (1807) and *The Essays of Elia* (1823), Lamb was an accountant in India House in London for more than 30 years. Among his friends were Wordsworth, Hazlitt, and Coleridge. His life was marked by tragedy and mental derangement. Never married (his affair with Ann Simmons came to nothing, which, according to E.V. Lucas, may have caused his short confinement in a mental asylum), Lamb was a caregiver for his sister Mary, who also used to suffer from insanity, more than him. In a fit of mania, she had stabbed their mother to death in 1796 but was spared imprisonment in view of her being mentally and psychologically disturbed. She was in and out of psychiatric facilities throughout her life.

Anyway, one of the great masters of the English essay and one of the most personal and intimate of the early 19th-century English essayists, Lamb's "New Year's Eve" essay is perhaps the most famous of its kind. In the essay, he reflects wistfully about the passage of time. Unlike those who look forward to the New Year, Lamb enjoys reminiscing about the past and staying at his present age of forty-five. Desiring to live with his books ("my midnight darlings") and familiar surroundings, he wishes neither to get older or younger nor to die:

> I am content to stand still at the age to which I am arrived; I and my friends: to be no younger, no richer, no handsomer. I do not want to be weaned by age; or drop, like mellow fruit...into the grave. Any alteration on this earth of mine, in diet or in lodging puzzles and discomposes me. My household-gods plant a terrible fixed foot, and are not rooted up without blood. They do not willingly seek Lavinian shores. A new state of being staggers me.

The sound of bells that says goodbye to the Old Year is "the most solemn and touching" to Lamb. This sound, nearest to heaven, makes him recall what has happened to him during the last twelve months. He breaks with his elders who observed the New Year according to old customs, rituals, and institutions. Unlike them, who rang out the Old Year with "ceremony" and "hilarity," the sound of the farewell midnight chimes always brings "a train of pensive imagery into his fancy." It is as if this were "a reckoning" for him.

From childhood till the age of thirty, a man is not concerned about his or human mortality. Although he may be aware of the fragility of life, he as a young man does not bring this awareness "home to himself." Lamb illustrates this with the analogy that although one knows about the shivering cold of winter, one can hardly appropriate it to his imagination in the hot June. However, as one grows older, one feels "these audits but too powerfully," counting every moment of life "like miser's farthings" but still failing to stop the unstoppable and that is the movement of "the great wheel" of time or the biblical "weaver's shuttle." Lamb's insight here anticipates what Thomas Hardy has to say in "At the Entering of the New Year," a poem Hardy wrote at the age of eighty in 1920, that when we are young we are not concerned about the passing of time because we know that there is always the new to come in and be celebrated, but when we are old we stem the tide of time as we then try to cling to the old as much as we can.

Lamb finds no solace in the "great wheel" and "weaver's shuttle" metaphors. He dismisses these as not "sweetening the unpalatable draught of mortality." He does not want "to be carried with the tide," even though that might "smoothly bear human life to eternity." He is reluctant at "the course of destiny," however inevitable that is. He wishes to defy the tide of time and does not want to submit to the inevitability of death because, in keeping with the Romantic environmental and ecological tradition, he says:

> I am in love with this green earth; the face of town and country; the unspeakable rural solitudes, and the sweet security of streets...Sun, and sky, and breeze, and solitary walks, and summer holidays, and the greenness of fields, and the delicious juices of meats and fishes, and society, and the cheerful glass, and candle-light, and fire-side conversations, and innocent vanities, and jests, and *irony itself*—do these things go out with life?

Like the opening sentences of Jane Austen's *Pride and Prejudice* and Dickens's *A Tale of Two Cities*, Lamb begins with one of the most famous and aphoristic openings in English prose—fictional or non-fictional. In contrast with the rest of the essay—intimate, playful, queer, quirky, wry, whimsical, archaic, pointed, and protean, as characterized by David Lazar—its beginning is less intimate, more formal and public, written in plain and simple English.[5] The very opening remark stresses the importance and lasting memorability of the New Year more than one's own birthday, which over time either lapses into disuse or loses its charm and significance:

> Every man hath two birth-days: two days, at least, in every year, which set him upon revolving the lapse of time, as it affects his mortal duration. The one is that which in an special manner he terms *his*. In the gradual disuse of old observances, this custom of solemnizing our proper birth-day hath nearly passed away, or is left to children, who reflect nothing at all about the matter, nor understand anything in it beyond cake and orange. But the birth of a New Year is of an interest too wide to be pretermitted by king or cobbler. No one ever regarded the First of January with indifference. It is that from which all date their time, and count upon what is left. It is the nativity of our common Adam.

On the New Year's eve, Lamb reminisces about his love saying he thinks it is better that he spent seven years of his prime languishing over—and being captivated by—the beauty of Ann Simmons, the relationship, however, never ending in marriage, than to have never experienced such a devoted and truly loving relationship:

> Methinks, it is better that I should have pined away seven of my goldenest years, when I was thrall to the fair hair and fairer eyes of [Ann Simmons] than that so passionate a love-adventure should be lost.

Lamb anticipates Tennyson, who says, in *In Memoriam* (1850), that "'Tis better to have loved and lost/ Than never to have loved at all." Similarly, he reflects about the financial inheritance from his father's will of which he has been cheated by one wicked William Dorrell, who was a witness to the will. Unlike his love affair, he thinks it would have been better for him to have missed the whole legacy and be without the idea of "that specious old rogue" than to have possessed a certain sum of money at present and suffer from the thought of being deprived.

Being without a wife or family, Lamb speculates that he cannot get out of himself, having thus developed the habit of turning back upon memory. He portrays himself as a man of "introspection," "retrospection," "self-love," "sickly idiosyncrasy," and self-ridicule but "impenetrable to ridicule" by others and beyond the sympathy of others. It is through "the phantom cloud" of Elia, his pseudonym after an Italian clerk, described as "a stammering buffoon," "a stupid changeling," that he has developed his persona. Lamb, in the guise of Elia, has finally evolved into a being of hope, honesty, courage, and imagination.

The New Year falls in winter, when nature is generally dead and which puts Lamb back in the contemplation mode about the correlation between him and nature. Lamb hates winter because it is in the cold, numbing winter that his thoughts of death—his "intolerable disinclination to dying"—return to haunt and beset him most. Winter blast "nips and shrinks" him. Like a snake which goes into hibernation in winter and comes back to activity in the summer, Lamb also enjoys a feeling of immortality in the summer as if death would not come to him then. By the same logic, he likes the sun (Phoebus/Apollo) and the light, warmth and vitality associated with it but he turns away from the moon (Diana/Artemis) and moonlight, which with their "shadowy and spectral appearances" (by way of a response to Coleridge's *Ancient Mariner*?), he thinks, are associated with cold and darkness. The moon is "the cold ghost of the sun, or Phoebus' sickly sister."

Lamb wants to continue an active and enjoyable life; he is not one of those who are indifferent to life and who welcome death "as a port of refuge and speak of the grave as of some soft arms, in which they may slumber as on a pillow." He shuns and proscribes death as a "foul, ugly phantom" and "a universal viper," to be detested, abhorred, and execrated. He also describes death as a "thin, melancholy *Privation*, or more frightful and confounding *Positive!*" that is only evil. He has a disgust at the "impertinent and misbecoming" tombstone inscriptions, which are no more than "frigid and insulting" antidotes against the fear of death. Patrick Madden finds Lamb's "New Year's Eve" "a perfect essay,"

> which in a spill of language and punctuation turns an occasion into a meditation, in this case on mortality, that inexhaustible topic and perennial favourite of writers from all ages. I love it for how it hooks not just my gut but my mind, not with drama or story but with idea, and because at nearly 200 years old, it still speaks to a universal feeling sparked by the arbitrary turning of the calendar leaf. Also because it reminds me, as any *memento mori* should, that I will die.[6]

By the end of the essay, Lamb moves from pondering over love, inheritance, and mortality to the state of feeling like a jolly man, alive and well, drinking happy drinks. His progress from emotional hurt to promise is like the midnight church bells, which, as a turncoat does, change their notes from mournful chanting about the departed year to "lustily" ringing in its successor—the New Year. Lamb quotes the poem by Cotton in full, which follows the same pattern, from hinting at the tormenting mischiefs and daily ills to welcoming the New Year with robust hopefulness. As he turns around, Lamb feels fortified as if he has drunk a comforting and pleasant-tasting drink that expands the heart and produces "sweet blood" (in contrast with the aching and numbing drink Keats drinks in the Nightingale Ode). He feels relieved ("washed," "cleansed" and "generous") by "the purging sunlight of clear poetry," referring to Cotton's cavalier poem and its smacking of "the magnanimity of the old English vein." With the reading of the poem by Cotton, "those puling fears of death" are gone like a cloud, finally making him wish many merry New Years to all.

Lamb re-employs, Gerald Monsman argues, Cotton's "mythological personification of the two-faced Janus as an emblem of Romantic synthesis.... As he warms with the delight of old poetry and the companionship of friends, Lamb is able to welcome the New Year with new-found self-esteem."[7] Lazar comments on Lamb's embracing of life in the end saying that his rebound from remorse and regret to promise, from pain to pleasure is funny, delightful and amusing. This transformation follows an alternating pattern of self-mocking, self-knowing, self-critical and self-comforting moments.

George William Curtis's "New Year" (January 1887) essay is perhaps the cutest and most accessible essay on the topic. It begins with a reference to Lamb's opening statement quoted above, that no one ever regarded the first of January with indifference. Regardless of how routine and punctual is the matter of the New Year and how no one had paid attention to it before Pope Gregory XIII and the British Parliament revised the Western calendar, there cannot be any loss of "the charm of regularly recurring times and seasons." Curtis goes on to say:

> Any day in any month, actually begins a new year, but that does not give to that date the significance and the feeling of the first of January. That is our day of remembrance, our feast of hope, the first page of our fresh calendar of good resolutions, the day of underscoring and emphasis of the swift lapse of life.

Curtis argues that the problems of white hairs, wrinkles, baldness, and eyesight are not necessarily marks of old age because they come to different people at different times, starting from young age. So it should not matter if one is at the threshold of fifty, sixty, or seventy. He says:

> Since, then, we cannot stop the flight of Time, let him pass. But he must not calumniate [make false or defamatory statements] as he passes. He must not be allowed to stigmatize vigor and health and freshness of feeling and the young heart and the agile foot as old merely because of a certain number of years. This is the season of good resolutions. The new year begins in a snow-storm of white vows. So be it. But let our whitest vow be, after that for a whiter life, that age shall no longer be measured by this arbitrary standard of years, and that those deceitful and practical octogenarians of thirty shall not escape as young merely because they have not yet shown the strength to carry three score and ten with jocund elasticity.

Fiona Macleod is the female pseudonym of the Scottish nature writer William Sharp. His beautiful, environmentally-aware "At the Turn of the Year," one of a/its kind, appeared in his collection of nature writings called *Where the Forest Murmurs* (1906). Reminding us of Lamb's love of his green surroundings, Macleod's ecologically more elaborate "green" and modern essay argues that nature never dies, not even in the deep, dead, and bleak December/January winter with its rains and storms. Nature continues to live in the form of "the coppice or by the stream-side, by the field-thicket, in the glens," and even on the wide moors under the "dense and wide" coverlet of sleet and snow. By no means nature can be thought of as lifeless at this season. There are winter plants, worms, insects, birds, and field-travellers such as the "resident and immigrant" larks,

> the wandering thrushes; the vagrant rooks, the barn-haunting hoodie; the yellow-hammer flocks and the tribes of the finch; the ample riverside life, where heron and snipe, mallard and moor-hen, wren and kingfisher, and even plover and the everywhere adaptable starling are to be found with ease by quick eyes and careful ears […] the sudden apparition of the bat, or the columnar dance of the ephemeridae [mayflies], or the flight of the winter-moth along the disheveled hedgerows […] the mistletoe and the ivy, the holly and the fir, the box and the late-flowering clematis, and many other of the green and flowering clans of the forest and the garden […] the midwinter-blooming [wild flower called] shepherd's purse, healing groundsel, bright chickweed, and red deadnettle […] the dun-hued lapwing […] the inland-wandering gull […].

Drawing an analogy of continuity with the one king dead and the incoming king wished to live long, Macleod asserts that "There is no interregnum" in nature, too. He is "a watcher of the multiform birdlife" of the "winter-fields and fallow lands" of Scotland, one who knows that "the same drama of life and death is enacted in midwinter as in midspring or midsummer, a drama only less crowded, less complex and less obvious, but not less continual, not less vital for the actors." Scottish landscape being the center of his attention, Macleod describes the impact of nature on it from all directions. He says that after the spring and summer cuckoos, swallows, landrails, and swans are gone by November by the effect of "the wet winds of the *west* and the freezing blasts of the *north*," "ten thousand wings" as "the migrants from overseas descend at last on our English and Scottish shores," starting from the autumn. A "myriad host," swept away, is replaced by "an incalculable host" due to "those *east* winds from Norway and the Baltic, from Jutland and Friesland, [...] those *south* winds leaping upward from the marshes of Picardy and the Breton heathlands and from all of the swarm-delivering South behind, [...] those *southwest* gales warm with the soft air of the isles of the west, and wet with the foam over lost Ys and sunken Lyonesse."

Turning to New Year poetry, Johann von Goethe wishes to forget the woe and anguish of the old year while expressing his zest and zeal for life, living every moment happily and rapturously in the company of friends during a merry New Year's party at his home in 1802. At the juncture of the departing and starting years, he recalls the cherished memories of the past moments but he also sees the future moments of joy and happiness at the change of the direction of the mysterious fate and fortune. It is both the prospects and problems and the prosperities and challenges that are suggested in his New Year's thoughts and prayers:

> Guide thro' life's mazy
> Pathways so hazy
> Into the year!

The occasion of Tennyson's musical "Ring out, wild bells" is the New Year's Eve of 1835 and then it was included in his elegiac masterpiece *In Memoriam* (1850). Like his widely known social and public voice in the context of the increasingly industrial and materialistic age, this song also is a generalized goodbye to all that is old and bad for the society and a hearty welcome to whatever is new and good for humankind:

Ring out the old, ring in the new,...
Ring out the false, ring in the true.
Ring out the grief that saps the mind,...
Ring out the feud of rich and poor,
Ring in redress to all mankind.
Ring out a slowly dying cause,
And ancient forms of party strife;
Ring in the nobler modes of life,
With sweeter manners, purer laws.
Ring out the want, the care, the sin,...
Ring out, ring out thy mournful rhymes,
But ring the fuller minstrel in.
Ring out false pride in place and blood,
The civic slander and the spite;
Ring in the love of truth and right,
Ring in the common love of good.
Ring out old shapes of foul disease,
Ring out the narrowing lust of gold;
Ring out the thousand wars of old,
Ring in the thousand years of peace.
Ring in the valiant man and free,
The larger heart the kindlier hand;
Ring out the darkness of the land,
Ring in the Christ that is to be.

Tennyson's "The Death of the Old Year," written in 1842, is completely different from his above poem. While in "Ring out, wild bells," he gives an impatient farewell to the old year and a fervent welcome to the New, "The Death of the Old Year" is a midnight lament for the old, which the poet does not want to die: "You came to us so readily/ You lived with us so steadily/ Old year you shall not die/... A jollier year we shall not see/... We did so laugh and cry with you." It was full of "joke and jest." Personified as a male friend, about to die by midnight and then dead at midnight and be shaken hands with before parting through dying, Tennyson personalizes "him" saying the old year was "a friend to me.... He gave me a friend and a true truelove," which the New Year, though "blithe and bold," will take away. The New Year is described as the old year's "son and heir," who steps in to take the place of the outgoing in the form of a corpse.

This is almost Dickinsonian. It is a characteristic of Emily Dickinson to give human qualities and attributes to non-human (animate or non-animate) objects and beings exactly as Tennyson does in his poem. She takes the opportunity of remembering her father's death a year prior in her "One Year Ago," written in memory of him and how graceful and glorious he was. Now that she is also old enough to die and so to wish for only one or still many more birthdays, she remembers her times with her father when she was young. Dickinson is, however, famous for her informal, conversational, and colloquial style, leaving more unsaid than said by means of her frequently used dashes, as Tennyson is, by contrast, for his smooth, rhythmic and musical style.

It is the similar materialistic and scientific 19th century, torn between faith and doubt, that has become a "century's corpse" and is being given a dull and mute farewell by the pessimistic Hardy in his "The Darkling Thrush," one of his most lyrical and anthologized poems:

The ancient pulse of germ and birth
    Was shrunken hard and dry,
And every spirit upon earth
    Seemed fervorless as I.

Probably written in the evening of December 31st, the poem was originally called "The Century's End, 1900".[8] It describes the last century as "bleak" and "broken," "cryptic" and "cloudy," and "frosty" and "specter-grey" as the December winter is. However, there is a hope with the "ecstatic" singing of a thrush, a Keatsian nightingale-like image:

At once a voice arose among
    The bleak twigs overhead
In a full-hearted evensong
    Of joy illimited;
An aged thrush, frail, gaunt, and small,
    In blast-beruffled plume,
Had chosen thus to fling his soul
    Upon the growing gloom.

Again, like Keats in "Ode to a Nightingale," Hardy is ambivalent and equivocal with the sense of joy being undercut because he hardly finds any cause in nature for the thrush to be so hopeful, yet he thinks, there may have "trembled through"

His happy good-night air
Some blessed Hope, whereof he knew
And I was unaware.

Hardy's second New Year poem, "New Year's Eve," was written in 1906 when he was about to be seventy. It is in the form of a philosophical or metaphysical dialogue between the poetic persona (of the agnostic Hardy) and God about the logic behind the creation of the earth from "formless void," an earth full of human suffering. God's reply is that it is for the humans not to see "the shortness of God's view" but to apply their reasons, their perceiving consciousness, as opposed to their sensory perceptions, to explain God's apparently "logicless" creation in an "unweeting" (unwitting or unknowing) way.

Hardy's third poem, "At the Entering of the New Year," was written on December 31, during the First World War (1914-18), when he was approaching eighty years of age. The poem is about the changing human attitude toward the New Year over the course of time from youth to old age. He says that while in youth he was careless about the passing of time, he was excited welcoming the New Year. In his older years, he experienced the losses of the First World War and so was attempting to stall the speed of time so that the memory of human cost and human heroism stayed longer with him, without letting it lapse into oblivion. At the beginning, WW I was full of high hopes about military and patriotic glory, but it proved to be shattering, full of prolonged violence and bloodshed that deeply impacted the psyche of the European younger generation.

However, the poem is not without its share of ambiguity and ambivalence, characteristic of Hardy. The Part I, introduced as "old style" and given in the past tense, describes the warm indoor celebration of the New Year by the young, whose songs and dances contrast with the cold and lonely darkness outside. Their throbbing delight is arousing to "home-gone husbandmen," "the white highway," "nighted farers," "shepherds at their midnight lambings," and "stealthy poachers." The youthful singing and dancing indoors is forgetful about the death and destruction writ large in the change of time:

As Time unrobed the Youth of Promise
Hailed by our sanguine sight.

Part II, in turn, is introduced as "new style" and is given in the simple present indefinite. It takes place in the evening, outside, when the tolling bells are "muffled" in the breeze. A "mantled ghost" seems to represent the "bereaved Humanity" in the context of the human suffering of WW I. It seeks to stop the "imminent," "mystic" New Year from coming: "Thy entrance here is undesired." Yet the New Year is addressed as "Calm comely Youth, untasked, untired," around which the "stars irradiate." Age wants the old time to delay its departure, yet it cannot wait to share in the appeal and excitement of the new:

Must we avow what we would close confine?
With thee, good friend, we would have converse none,
Albeit the fault may not be thine.

Age may lament the ravages of time, but it cannot completely turn its back on the charm of the fresh start of a New Year. Similarly, just as the early enthusiasm for the glory of war tended to sideline the suffering and death it would inevitably bring, the slowly but surely surfacing war weariness and resistance to war could not hide the admiration for the courage and valor of the battlefield. Hardy's "At the Entering of the New Year" looks back and looks forward to all the war memories in history—ancient or modern, colonial or postcolonial, especially on the Veterans (or Remembrance) Day that is observed around the world on November 11 to honor the fallen and the wounded or all men and women that served in the military. Hardy's poem no doubt reflects what many try to balance that day: honoring the veterans while remembering the losses caused by war. As Judy Foster comments, even the pacifist protesting against the war gives homage to those who gave their lives or got wounded in the service to their country. Hardy's poem is, therefore, "no simple protest against time or change or war, but a reflection on the ambiguity of human experience, whether in youth or age, at war or at peace."[9]

The American Romantic poet William Cullen Bryant's "A Song for New Year's Eve" (1859), though unique and uncommon, sounds like Tennyson's "The Death of the Old Year." It looks back to the past year, personified as a generous male being of benign soul, not as one that was full of sorrow and suffering. It was "the good old year/ So long companion of our way." Bryant says he should be "grateful" and "mirthful" at this last "golden" hour of the past year, "The kindly year [whose] liberal hands/ Have lavished all his store" and when,

Days brightly came and calmly went,
  While yet he was our guest;

How cheerfully the week was spent!
How sweet the seventh day's rest!

At this "tender" hour when the passing year is about to leave with his "last smile," the poet remembers "the pleasant memories" of those who died last year and wishes the New Year to be as kind. With nostalgia, he is asking his friends to stay "one hour more of jest and song" or one more "little" hour to sing a "parting strain."

Bryant's contemporary Helen Hunt Jackson's "New Year's Morning" is one of the most inspirational and motivating New Year poems. A prelude to New Year's Eve, the poem is about "the annoying expression of the 'old year' that not only frets over its fate, but is also jealous of the new chances brought by the New Year." It is futile to fret over what could have been done in the days gone by and it is the same to blame fate for all that may have gone wrong in the course of the last year. Instead, the New Year's morning is a time for new endeavours. The poem is a reminder of the opportunities that each day as a new day brings along with it, implying that each day is to be lived fully without letting it go by otherwise.

While there is a sense of glitz and glamor about the evenings, which suggest a time of fun and partying with family and friends, especially if it is the New Year's Eve, mornings are for the new serious efforts and undertakings. As the New Year comes in with new opportunities, there is a chance to make it "big"—successful and productive—all over again. Instead of crying over the spilt milk, as the critic says, the poet encourages humankind to take each day as a new beginning and reach out for the stars. The personified Old Year says:

The blossoms of the New Year's crown
Bloom from the ashes of the dead…
By all my failures it shall learn.
I have been reckless; it shall be
Quiet and calm and pure of life.
I was a slave; it shall go free,
And find sweet pace where I leave strife.

Referring to the New Year's Eve in particular and every night in general as "the healing balm of sleep," Jackson is wondering how "Only a night from old to new" brings all the changes and miracles:

Each morn is New Year's morn come true,
Morn of a festival to keep.

All nights are sacred nights to make
Confession and resolve and prayer;
All days are sacred days to wake
New gladness in the sunny air.
Only a night from old to new;
Only a sleep from night to morn.
The new is but the old come true;
Each sunrise sees a new year born.

Tennyson's "Ring out, wild bells" foreshadows an equally generalized and fervent farewell to the age-old burden of evil and a lofty call to the new and fresh to take hold as the 1913 Bengali Nobel laureate Rabindranath Tagore welcomes the Bengali New Year *Pohela Boishakh* (1st day of the first month of the Bengali calendar, *Boishakh*) in his "Esho hey Boishakh esho esho" (Come, O Boishakh, come, come). Tagore was inspired to write many poems and songs to greet the Bengali New Year, which, unlike the West, heralds amid the great variety of spring colours and various weather patterns, from moderate to warm, hot and humid, sometimes accompanied by strong winds and heavy showers, even storms and cyclones. All these are hinted at by Tagore in the following beautiful New Year lyric, which in a way reads like Shelley's *West Wind*:

LIKE FRUIT, shaken free by an impatient wind
from the veils of its mother flower,
thou comest, New Year, whirling in a frantic dance
amid the stampede of the wind-lashed clouds
and infuriate showers,
while trampled by thy turbulence
are scattered away the faded and the frail
in an eddying agony of death.
Thou art no dreamer afloat on a languorous breeze,
lingering among the hesitant whisper and hum
of an uncertain season.
Thine is a majestic march, o terrible Stranger,
thundering forth an ominous incantation,
driving the days on to the perils of a pathless dark,
where thou carriest a dumb signal in thy banner,
a decree of destiny undeciphered.[10]

India being a large country of colourful cultural, linguistic, and seasonal diversity, there is no single Hindu New Year, although there is the Indian

National calendar. Therefore, different parts of the country such as West Bengal, Gujarat, Kerala, Karnataka, Andhra Pradesh, Sind, and Central India celebrate the New Year in different ways at different times of the year. In Gujarat, the New Year festival coincides with the Hindu religious festival of Diwali, the festival of (little oil) lamps to welcome Goddess Lakshmi, the Goddess of riches.

Unlike many poets discussed above, D.H. Lawrence strikes a very personal longing for passionate, sensual love in his "New Year's Eve" and "New Year's Night" poems:

Take off your things.
Your shoulders, your bruised throat!
Your breasts, your nakedness!
As the darkness flickers and dips,
As the firelight falls and leaps
From your feet to your lips!

In consonance with the "animal vibrance" that is there in all his works, Lawrence describes his beloved as a white dove in his arms, "bought at great price" and "worth more than all I've got." The New Year's night is the time for her innocence, purity, and virginity to be sacrificed through sexual initiation, thereby their mutual "Pride, strength, all the lot" to be yielded. The beloved is actually treated like an object of sacrificial offering in the possession of the lover who, in the face of inescapable mortality, intends to put her on the altar of death, "the ancient, inexorable God." The sudden unexpectedness of death is such that, Lawrence says in the poem, it swoops down on the victim like a falcon. It seems he suggests that it is through an intense sexual experience that time and death can be overcome and overpowered. The similes and images of the dove, sacrifice, the pain of loss, and death, all thought about at the New Year, provide a philosophical perspective and spiritual context for the vigor and warmth of human sexuality taken beyond the realm of physicality in a characteristically Lawrentian way. The two short lyrics manage to explore "a range of emotions, from exhilaration to depression to prophetic brooding."

The thought of "New Year on Dartmoor" by Sylvia Plath came to her as she, pregnant with her second child, was out for a walk from their (she and Ted Hughes) 11th century manor house on the Devon moor with her small (one-and-a-half-year-old) daughter, sometime in late December 1961. It was just over a year before her suicide at the age of thirty in her fragile and then shattering relationship with Hughes. The poem describes the New Year in a highly metaphoric and unrealistic way. The little child in all her innocence is amazed and excited by the "newness" of the icy New Year winter scene. She is overjoyed to see all the ice sparkle over the ordinary ("tawdry") things around. However, the mother, sadly, knows that all the nearby gleaming and glowing that are there are short lasting and deceiving and that the only truth that lies behind the gaudy glitter is the challenges and hardships that the New Year brings with it.

> This is newness: every little tawdry
> Obstacle glass-wrapped and peculiar,
> Glinting and clinking in a saint's falsetto. Only you
> Don't know what to make of the sudden slippiness,
> The blind, white, awful, inaccessible slant.
> There's no getting up it by the words you know.
> No getting up by elephant or wheel or shoe.
> We have only come to look. You are too new
> To want the world in a glass hat.

There is a long list of New Year poems and essays to recall on 31 December and 1 January. The above is just a selection from many. Other poems would include "New Year's Day Nap" by Coleman Barks, "The Old Year" by John Clare, "On a New Year's Eve" by June Jordan, "The Passing of the Year" and "New Year's Eve" by Robert W. Service, "A New Year's Day Poem" by Charles Moir, "A New Year's Gift" by William Strode, "A New Year's Resolution to Leave Dundee" by William Topaz McGonagall, "My New Year's resolution" by Robert Fisher, "New Year Poem" by Barry Tebb, and "New Year's Chimes" by Francis Thompson. Although the subject is the same, like love and religion, every composition, be it a poem or a piece of prose, is different with different themes and ideas. All are not only interesting but striking as well, suggesting the endless and inexhaustible beauty and variety of the New Year reflections and reactions.

NOTES

1. "Christianity found that a number of Celtic customs were compatible with their religion and hence adopted them. The Church adopted Samhain as the Feast of All Saints or Hallow Tide and Oidhche Shamhna became Halloween."

2. Visit http://www.indobase.com/holidays/new-year/newyear-in-different-religions/

   Like the Christian and the Celtic customs, there are similarities between the Arabic and the Jewish ones, too. The Jewish calendar, like the Arabic calendar, is based on the moon cycles, not the sun cycles. Both Arabic and Jewish New Years coincide and are compatible with each other, coming about the same time. Both Islam and Judaism being monotheistic and sharing similar religious history and beliefs, both the tenth of Muharram (*Ashura*) and the tenth of Tishri (*Yom Kippur*) are profoundly holy to Muslims and Jews, respectively with many religious events from time immemorial believed to have occurred on this tenth, so that both communities fast the whole day on the day, with Muslims actually preferring to fast two days, either Muharram 9 and 10 or 10 and 11 because of the problems connected with moon sighting and also to differentiate their practice from the Jews. It is to be mentioned here that "The *Hebrew calendar* is a luni-solar *calendar*, meaning that months are *based on lunar* months, but years are *based* on solar years," starting from the Passover that commemorates the Exodus of the people of Israel from ancient Egypt, so that the Gregorian/Christian 2015-16 coincides with the Hebrew 5776.
3. http://poetry.about.com/od/ourpoemcollections/a/newyearpoems.htm
4. In classical times, poets were crowned with a laurel wreath (emblems of a poet). The Italian Francis Petrarch (1304-74) contrived to have himself crowned "poet laureate." Chaucer's Clerk refers to Petrarch as "lauriat poete" in *The Clerk's Tale*, which is based on Petrarch's Latin version of the last tale of Boccaccio's *Decameron*. There is the poet Cuddie in Spenser's *The Shepherd's Calendar* (tenth eclogue/October), which deals with the place of poetry and the responsibility of the poet in the world, an important theme throughout much of Spenser's work. Although there is no formal job description, it is understood that poets laureate are required to write verses about the royal family and on grand national and ceremonial occasions. The job of the poet laureate (the monarch's pensioned poet) has in the past been a lifetime appointment with an annual honorarium of £100 a year, but in a departure from custom, Britain has recently said that the appointment, starting from Andrew Motion, would be for 10 years and that there would be an annual payment of £5000. The appointment is approved by the queen but chosen from a short list by the British Prime Minister. British poets laureate include John Skelton, who was the major poet of the first quarter of the 16th century, with the title of poet laureate from both Oxford and Cambridge. In 1616, Ben Jonson was appointed poet laureate with a pension of a handsome amount, the first such appointment in English literary history. He rose from humble beginnings to become England's unofficial poet laureate with a substantial

pension from the king and honorary degrees from both Oxford and Cambridge. William Davenant was poet laureate from 1637-50 (then not knighted). John Dryden held the title for twenty years until 1670 when he was deprived of it by the Catholic James II for his earlier allegiance to James's Stuart brother Charles II at the Restoration. There were Thomas Shadwell, until his death in 1692; Nahum Tate, 1693 to 1715; Thomas Warton the Younger, 1785-90; H.J. Pye, from 1790; Robert Southey, 1831-to his death in 1843; Wordsworth, 1843 to his death in 1850; Tennyson, 1850-92 (no new poet-laureate was appointed for four years after Tennyson's death); Alfred Austin, 1896-1912; Robert Bridges, 1913-30; C. Day-Lewis, John Masefield, John Betjeman, Ted Hughes (from 1985), Andrew Motion, 1999-2009, and Carol Ann Duffy. Thomas Gray declined the offer of poet laureate in 1757; Walter Scott was offered the honor in 1813 but he declined and recommended Southey; Samuel Rogers, William Morris, and Rudyard Kipling refused. The American poet laureate position was established by an act of Congress in 1985. Robert Penn Warren, Richard Wilbur, Mark Strand, Joseph Brodsky, Robert Pinsky, and Rita Dove were among the American poets laureate.

5. David Lazar, "Reading 'New Year's Eve,'" in *Understanding the Essay*, eds. Patricia Foster and Jeff Porter (Peterborough, Ontario: Broadview Press, 2012), pp. 206-17.
6. http://www.essaydaily.org/2012/12/dec-31-patrick-madden-on-charles-lambs.html
7. https://www.questia.com/library/journal/1G1-188997958/charles-lamb-as-the-janus-of-romanticism-in-new-year-s
8. "A deleted 1899 on the manuscript suggested he had written it a year before," Claire Tomalin tells us in her biography of Hardy, *Thomas Hardy: The Time-Torn Man* (Viking Penguin, 2006).
9. http://yourbrainonbooks.blogspot.com/2011/01/at-entering-of-new-year-by-thomas-hardy_01.html
10. From *The English Writings of Rabindranath Tagore*, ed. Sisir Kumar Das (Sahityo Akademi, New Delhi: 2004), p. 320.

The Sufi Impact: Doris Lessing's Quest for Perennial Values

ANITA MYLES

DORIS LESSING (1919-2013), the Nobel Laureate of 2007 and one of the most intensely committed writers among the contemporary English novelists emits an ardent desire to redeem society from the various deterrent forces simultaneously endeavouring to evolve a social system which would be of universal import. Lessing is not a philosopher nor does she advocate any particular school of thought but merely attempts to asseverate the quintessence of her lifelong experiences for the benefit of her readers. Though conscious of society's hostility to a person who tends to offer a newer and perhaps a better alternative as a solution to various problems, her belligerent spirit prevents her from surrendering to the societal pressures.

Steeped in controversy right from her first novel, *The Grass is Singing* (1950) and her first collection of short stories, *The African Stories* (1964) Doris Lessing initially encountered immense condemnation, criticism and ostracization due to her revolutionary views focusing on racial injustices, alignment towards communism and projecting Marxian idea of religion being the opium of the masses, eventually being declared a '*persona non grata*' by the British Government for quite some time. Nevertheless, with great grit and determination the novelist proceeded with her writing proffering bold statements about apartheid highlighting other social issues like women liberation, discussing negative role of religion in its attempt to suppress intellectual freedom and resorting to political condemnation of England's decision to manufacture the hydrogen bomb through participation in the famous 'Aldermaston March'. However, her search for establishing stability in human life throughout the world culminated in accepting the Sufi doctrine of mental evolution in which all God's creations—animals, plants and human beings are accepted equally significant parts of the Divine scheme. In this sense,

Lessing's diversion to Sufism becomes a necessary step in understanding her novelistic evolution.

Lessing's fiction may be studied under four distinct phases:

1. The African theme (1950-64)
2. The Communist theme (1965-68)
3. The Psychological theme (1969-72)
4. The Sufi theme (1973 onwards)

It must be comprehended at this stage that problems related to apartheid continued to haunt her right up to her first novel of *Canopus in Argos: Archives* series entitled *Shikasta* whereas traces of Sufism began filtering in her work as early as 1950.

Due to the astonishing multiplicity of themes ingrained in her novels, she has been variously dubbed as an African writer, a Communist writer, a feminist writer, a mystic writer, a psychological writer and a science-fiction writer. However, a steady progression in her thought pattern from Communism to Sufism is noticeable. In fact, this intellectual journey of the author has been called "her personal Pilgrim's Progress".

During the first decade of her creative excursion, Doris Lessing dealt with a variety of social problems and corrupt practices the emphasis being largely on racialism, generation gap, sexual re-adjustment, marital maladjustments and women liberation. Initially, her efforts to proffer solutions to these problems were catervaulted, though subsequently she succeeded in finding a way out of these mires. In her well-known 'Quintet', *The Children of Violence* she considered Communism as a possible alternative, which however was inappropriate. She then began to concentrate on the theme of women liberation and expressed her ideas in the *magnum opus The Golden Notebook* (1962). While analyzing the ordeals faced by the twentieth-century Western women, she points out the futility of 'sexual liberty' sought by them concluding in favour of the idea of women being subordinated to men. Doris Lessing divulged that all her female protagonists consciously attempted to attain self-identity and failing in this mission they suffered from frustration leading to nervous breakdown, self-division and schizophrenia.

While dealing with these theme Doris Lessing read two books which influenced her greatly: Rushbrook Williams' *Sufi Studies: East and West* and Idries Shah's *Tales of the Dervish*. Undoubtedly, Lessing's birth in Iran to English parents and her upbringing in Southern Rhodesia moulded her into a sort of spiritual ambassador between the East and the West. Through her writings, she introduced contemporary Western readers to ideas and literature from the Muslim world—something they were largely unaware of till then, convinced that Sufi studies and teaching could be a possible alternative to Western conditioning. The inclusion of the Sufi aspect in Lessing's works made her approach to life didactic as much as literary. During her thirty-year apprenticeship to Idries Shah, she was impressed by the Dervishes who led frugal lives and by their austerity and devotion developed higher mental concentration enabling them to communicate with other Dervishes telepathically. She also read *The Sufis*, another book by Idries Shah which claimed that humanity is forever evolving and hence there is a possibility of 'a conscious evolution' and 'a rarefied evolution'. In *Walking in the Shade*, an autobiographical piece, published in 1997, she referred to Sufism as "the main current in my life, deeper than any other, my real preoccupation." Gradually, she attempted to master the tenets of Sufism which would be used not only for her personal contentment but also for the benefit of the world at large realizing that man has the capability of transforming life by his conscious efforts utilizing this power later to serve mankind by venturing on the path of planned evolution.

A fundamental concept in Sufism is the idea that the seeker has direct access to God with no intermediary; that is, inner transformation can only be experienced, not discussed. An equally central notion is the idea of developing a person's potential. Sufism advocates love and tolerance—virtues which can bring harmony and interconnectedness to all forms of organic life. It is intrinsic, claims Doris Lessing, to experience Sufism in order to enjoy and understand it to the core. One can never get a perfect knowledge of Sufi ideology through books alone; it has to be practiced. In order to develop a superior consciousness and to develop fellow feelings genuinely for other human beings one has to transcend the mundane only then noble thoughts will enter his mind. This was Lessing's purpose when she became inclined towards Sufism. She had been endeavouring to search for peace and perfection in various philosophies and metaphysics but ultimately it was Sufism that emerged as a comforting spiritual alternative without damaging her own Christian beliefs. Lessing was apparently impressed by Sufism as it imbibed the essence of every religion and was allured by the claim of Idries Shah that Sufism is a sophisticated view of life, fundamentally embodied in people who through centuries have always been in advance of their time.

The idea of Sufism lurked in her mind ever since she had left Rhodesia. Dee Seligman aptly points out:

> Since then Doris Lessing has written frequently about the impact of Sufism in her personal life and this form of mysticism figures critically in her later works. At some point along her long journey away from friends and homeland, Doris Lessing found a technique and vocabulary which she might have discovered years ago. But she had to go a solitary route before she had made such a discovery.
>
> (*Modern Fiction Studies*, 14)

Seligman's remark is justified as the mature novels are perceptibly coloured by her Sufi ideology. Undoubtedly, to Lessing Sufi philosophy opened up new vistas of perusing life enabling her to offer greater faith and hope in her novels than she dispensed earlier. Her radical departure from the secularized world view of the twentieth-century West distinguishes her from other Western contemporary writers. She learnt from Sufism how to fully develop and balance all available faculties so that human beings can disengage themselves from destructive prejudices and stubborn notions thus evading catastrophe. In this sense for her Sufism was the "ancient way to new freedom".

At this stage Doris Lessing ascertained that she was better placed to provide some alternatives to problems instead of just enumerating them. She also develops a definite precept of life clearly indicating towards cosmic welfare for which advocating self-therapy she postulates that men and women themselves are responsible for their miseries and hence can be rid of them by their conscious efforts. She emphasizes in the 'Preface' to *The Golden Notebook* that the main theme is breakdown resulting in unity and not woman liberation. Several incidents in the novel reveal that Anna Wulf, the protagonist is a split personality on the verge of a nervous breakdown. She meets Saul Green, an American also experiencing a similar breakdown. Consequently, they interact, unveil their problems, are drawn close together, finally, understanding the shocking truth that the most destructive aspect of the human personality is its subjectivity. Doris Lessing justifies her inference through the following statement:

> The theme of 'breakdown', that sometimes when people 'crack up', it is a way of self-healing, of the inner self's dismissing false dichotomies and divisions....
>
> (*The Golden Notebook*, p. viii)

Thus, she avers that egocentricity must be completely effaced and annihilated as a part of self-therapy. Desiring the emancipation of the individual from the prison of self, she creates a mobile image to express the phenomenon in a more extensive manner—the body floating out of the confinement of the four walls of a room.

The novelist perpetually explores the latent potentialities of man, that how much the individual is prepared and capable of successfully effacing the self which, once again, evidenced her interest in Sufism. One of her statements emphatically reiterates this idea:

> Man is woefully underused and undervalued and does not know his own capacities. I have believed this all my life and that the idea is central to Sufism is one reason I was attached to it.
>
> (*The Elephant in the Dark*, 78)

Lessing was all along conscious of the impact of Sufism on her works basically through the writings of Idries Shah. In a letter to Roberta Rubenstein, she wrote:

> Man has the possibility of conscious self-development, becoming able—with his own efforts and under certain kind of expert guidance—to transcend ordinary limitations: this not for 'kicks' or for self-aggrandizement, but to serve mankind on its path of planned evolution.
>
> (Letter, March 28, 1977)

The extract distinctly indicates that man can resort to act in a manner worthwhile for the entire humanity substantiating Lessing's progression from the microcosm to the macrocosm.

This particular concept of conscious evolution finds emphatic expression in *The Four-Gated City* (1969). Martha Quest, the thirty-year-old protagonist confronts multiple experiences culminating in her emotional, sexual, intellectual and psychic evolution. Witnessing the emergence of spiritual sterility induced by war she develops a deep concern for the people living a life of constant emotional strain. While sojourning in the house of Mark Coleridge she acquires greater maturity developing better consciousness. The concluding part of the novel reveals a movement towards Sufi mysticism. Martha eventually convinces Mark to compose a novel entitled *A City in the Desert* sharing with him her own dream of an ideal city—'the New Jerusalem' a C*ivitas Dei* much akin to a utopia.

Martha Quest is portrayed having consciously developed telepathic power and can easily 'tune in' to other people's 'wavelength'. In this process of psychological plenum, Martha gets emotionally closer to Lynda, Mark's wife, who is suffering from a nervous breakdown and is branded as insane but actually she lives in a state of heightened consciousness. Martha spends a month in the basement with Lynda finally bringing her quest to a successful culmination. Emerging from the basement, a completely transformed woman, Martha is filled with 'an effulgence of light' feeling to be in complete unison with the outer world. Martha's attainment of superior consciousness proves Lessing's orientation towards Sufism. In *The Four-Gated City*, Doris Lessing, while commenting on Idries Shah explains Sufism as follows:

> Sufis believe that, expressed in one way, humanity is evolving towards a certain destiny, we are all taking part in that evolution. The difference between all evolutions is that for the last ten thousand years or so we have been given the possibility of a conscious evolution. So essential is this more rarefied evolution that our future depends on it.
>
> (1971, 'Preface', Part III)

Doris Lessing assimilates this thought in the 'Appendix' of the novel. A span of two decades gets quickly unfolded through letters and telepathic communications narrating about the survival of seventy-three persons on an uncontaminated island who have escaped a nuclear holocaust. This new generation is not only physically healthy but is also endowed with a higher range of superior consciousness. These survivors are, in reality, the mutants entrusted with the task of producing a new race. The island obviously symbolizes Martha's 'New Jerusalem' which she has been questing for all along.

Martha attempts to 'resurrect her lost past' for the sake of survival realizing the ultimate truth about heightened consciousness when she exclaims, "I am what the human race is!" In other words, she now moves closer to identifying her microcosmic individualism with the macrocosmic universality. In the final section of the novel, she is revealed to be standing alone and her ultimate realization of the self finds expression in the form of following question-answer:

> Where? But where? How? Who: No, but where, where?....Here, where else, you fool, you poor fool, where else has it been, ever.
>
> (*The Four-Gated City*, 591)

Martha's outburst is not irrational but proclaims the basic Sufi faith that the individual must find answers to his inner dissonance in his own actions, behaviour and mental potency instead of probing unsuccessfully here and there.

Charles Watkins, the protagonist of Doris Lessing's *Briefing for a Descent into Hell* (1971) encounters a similar situation. Watkins, a Cambridge classics professor loses his memory, spends three months in a psychiatric hospital on drugs which induce hallucinations, staying in a perpetual state of chaos and self-division but instead of losing hope, endeavours to overcome the final split. Watkins, a schizoid embarks on a number of 'metamorphic and symbolic journeys', quite akin to R.D. Laing's description of a schizophrenic. Laing contented that such patients go through a process of self-healing initially experiencing psychotic breakdown, though this journey is never destructive. However, there is a difference. Laing's patients restrict themselves to self-healing whereas Lessing's Watkins is concerned not only with himself but also with cosmic welfare and after reaching psychic plenum moves a step further in cultivating superior consciousness.

During one of his sea journeys Watkins notices a strange unearthly light, which the novelist calls the 'Crystal'. The 'Crystal' disappears with his shipmates leaving him alone. Watkins, then undertakes an inner space journey struggling to reach the "Crystal again but it also recapitulates the cumulative history of life on earth" (Rubenstein, 180). Lessing further delineates Watkins in conjugation with the first living organism that emerges from the slime as they become land creatures, a process highly symbolic indicating the emergence of human consciousness in its progression towards wholeness. Such a synthesis of the spiritual and the biological phases of evolution is adapted from the writings of Jallaluddin Rumi, the thirteenth-century Sufi teacher. Watkins prepares a clean landing place for the 'Crystal', though the landing of the 'Crystal' results in disappointment for him because he is not properly 'tuned in'. Describing this process as the development of superior consciousness Idries Shah writes:

> Every fibre has been purified, raised to a higher state, vibrates to a higher tune, gives out a more direct, more penetrating note....
>
> (1971, 122-23)

The Sufis believe that a proper 'tuning in' can be invariably attained through necessary mental purification which, in the course of time, brings inner transformation. Watkins' evolutionary ascent towards higher consciousness is indicated when he propels upwards with the help of a great white bird. Watkins is now 'a renewed man' for he has benefitted by his inner conflict and is well prepared when the 'Crystal' comes again to receive him. Some other writers and thinkers have also explained this kind of spiritual illumination. Evelyn Underhill refers to it as the "Crystallization of consciousness at a higher level" (*Mysticism*, 135), while Idries Shah interprets it as follows:

> When apparent opposites are reconciled, the individuality is not only complete, it also transcends the bounds of ordinary humanity as we can state it to be immensely powerful.
>
> (1971, 142)

Doris Lessing, too, holds the firm conviction that such a spiritual realization amounts to a sort of victory for the individual, no doubt, but is equally essential for the common weal.

Lessing's attitude reiterates the idea of Laing, who claimed,

> Cracked mind of the schizophrenic may let in light which does not enter the intact minds of many sane people whose minds are closed.
>
> (*The Divided Self*, 130)

The novelist expresses a similar thought in *Briefing for a Descent into Hell* describing the patients residing in mental hospitals as "millions who have cracked making cracks where the light could shine through at last" (130). Sufi's love and concern equally for the entire creation gets reflected in this pronouncement of Lessing when instead of condemning the mentally disabled persons she visualizes hope of betterment for them.

In order to formulate a proper vision of life Lessing draws inspiration from Sufism and some psychological theorists realizing that they lay immense importance on mental power eventually assimilating this idea into her own system of 'self-therapy' and 'mental pathology'. Her meticulous experimentation with the system of self-healing continues in the novel *The Summer before the Dark* (1973). Kate, the protagonist of this novel utters a significant statement, "We are what we learn". A person may have a split personality but with maturity he becomes more receptive. Consequently, the process of psychic integration and mental plenum appears a definite possibility.

The novelist renders an extremely practical view of life through the external experiences as well as introspection of Kate who faces her domestic responsibilities as a wife and a mother courageously and in spite of reaching the brink of mental disaster several times, retains her composure and arrives at the conclusion that she must not only sustain others but also preserve her own individuality. Whereas Watkins journeys only through stages of both amnesia and anamnesia successively, Kate is able to achieve psychic plenum only because she has an enhanced desire for liberty and tranquillity: "one last effort and I shall be free. Freedom and peace, how I have longed for you both" (*The Summer before the Dark,* 159).

Kate's yearning for 'wholeness' provides her 'mental synthesis' which tends to be one of the basic ideas pursued by the novelist. This synthesis is possible only at an extremely high level of consciousness and is same as the Sufi principle of the merger of microcosm into macrocosm resulting in the proliferation of organic sensibility. Sufis visualize a unity in all creations and have equal concern for animals, birds, water creatures and human beings. In the novel *The Summer before the Dark*, Kate's inner struggle is exhibited through a symbolic dream in which she locates a dying seal and attempts to save it by carrying it to the sea. This dream, apart from representing a longing for independent existence, has another significance in Lessingian pattern. Kate's concern for the seal can be equated with the concern shown by some characters in other novels of Lessing for animal welfare like Hugo in *The Memoirs of a Survivor* (1974) and Watkins' association with various animals in *Briefing for a Descent into Hell.* This envisages the novelist's dream of a golden age in which animals and human beings will coexist, definitely a Sufi concept conveying the idea of the fusion of life in its totality and the survival of noble emotions.

Once again the impact of the Sufi view of psychic evolution is evident on Doris Lessing's extensive use of 'Rooms' and 'Walls' as recurring symbols in many of her novels. Various characters attempt to break through the walls which signify barriers in their evolutionary process. The osmosis beyond the walls is more psychological than physical and postulates the shift from the exterior to the interior dimensions of experience. The 'Narrator' of the story in *The Memoirs of a Survivor* travels beyond the walls observing vacant rooms lying in need of repair. The disordered rooms symbolize the chaos existing in the 'Narrator's' own consciousness. At the outset the 'Narrator' is shocked but gradually compromises to each revelation, prepared to regulate the chaos within her and also visualizing a happy future for all. Finally, the 'Narrator's' efforts are rewarded and the boundary between the inner self and the outer self appearing to be unconquerable so far, dissolves at the moment of spiritual gnosis resulting in a complete and wilful escape from the prison of self-cultivating a wider perspective of human welfare. *The Memoirs of a Survivor*, according to Lessing, is "a kind of autobiography". It postulates the theme of shift from the exterior to the interior dimension of experience converging on the Sufi view of psychic evolution. The main theme of the novel focuses on the 'Narrator's' effort at mending the damage beyond the wall in which she fails initially. This continuous effort symbolizes the gradual evolution of consciousness in its journey towards fresh self-recognition. Later, when the vision of the room disappears she explains it in terms of the Sufi doctrine of self-realization that the room "had not disappeared, and the work in it continued, must continue, would go on always" (*The Memoirs of a Survivor*, 70). Such processes are analyzed and explained also by Freud, Jung and Laing but Doris Lessing in her letter to Roberta Rubenstein claims:

> Ibn El Arabi and El Ghazzah, in the Middle Ages, had more developed ideas about this "unconscious", collective or otherwise, than Jung, among others. He was a limited man.
>
> (Letter dated March 28, 1977)

Perceptibly, the novelist firmly believed that the philosophy of abnormal psychologists and leading psychiatrists was much truncated and under-developed in comparison to the Sufi doctrine.

The novel culminates on a highly symbolic note about which Rubenstein appropriately comments:

> The ending of *The Memoirs of a Survivor* is a rendering into language an image of the essentially ineffable experience of transcendence—the state of elevated consciousness characteristic of the mystical experience, whether conceived as a union with the deity, dissolution of ego boundaries, *Sotori,* enlightenment, illumination, or apotheosis.
>
> (*The Novelistic Vision*, 1979, 237)

The Memoirs of a Survivor is undoubtedly, Doris Lessing's fullest expression of the Sufi belief in the 'conscious attainment of self-purification'.

While composing *The Four-Gated City,* Lessing was deeply influenced by Sufi thought, but in *The Memoirs of a Survivor* the impact becomes persistent and prominent because the recurrent theme in her novels from now onwards acquires a definite shape in the form of the 'conscious attainment of self-purification'. Another noteworthy fact is that Doris Lessing combined with Sufi doctrines the principles of Jung and Laing as well, which encouraged her to include metaphysical themes in her fiction. Beginning her writing for the welfare of a limited group that is the Africans, subsequently she attempted for universal well-being and finally concentrates on a wider horizon that is cosmic harmony. With a view to achieving this objective, Lessing created her own cosmology and in a series of five novels entitled *Canopus in Argos: Archives* she reveals this cosmic consciousness in a clearer and more definite form. This series itinerates the readers through prehistoric, historic, modern and postmodern periods transversing the limits of time and space questing for a golden age where there would be peace and harmony. The novelist envisages a fanciful paradise in the imaginative reconstruction of various Biblical episodes conjoining them rationally with medieval Christian philosophy, Sufi doctrines and recent scientific discoveries.

Lessing's vision of the future formulates history as a process of redemption shattering the conventional barriers which consider man as a sinner, who, in order to attain deliverance, must pass through purgation; still, it is doubtful whether salvation would be bestowed. Her system begins with this idea no doubt, but her prophetic vision under the influence of Sufism tends to be more positive and practical than the traditional Christian doctrine. She suppeditates the future with a hope of mutating into a world spirit discerned by her as 'Cosmic Harmony'. Thus, the principal object of Lessing's historic vision is that life is an upward journey leading to the emancipation of the entire mankind. Lessing takes man as the medium of history and shows his cosmic voyage moving from ego to egolessness bringing real self-knowledge. So the central figures in her novels represent the alliance of levity and seriousness directed towards the awakening of a spirit animating the cosmic scale of life which she terms 'Conscious Evolution'.

Shikasta (1979), the first novel of the series *Canopus in Argos: Archives* manifests the perennial theme of perpetual confrontation between the forces of good and evil claiming that it is entirely in the hands of a person to shun evil and by the process of conscious evolution to bring about the golden age. In the novels of Doris Lessing, the concept that the attainment of superior consciousness brings harmony is symbolized by geometrical cities. The vision of cities recurs in several of her novels such as *Martha Quest* (1952), *The Four-Gated City* and *Shikasta*. The image of geometrical cities has been further extended and elaborated in *Marriages Between Zones Three, Four and Five* (1980), the second novel in the series *Canopus in Argos: Archives*. In this novel, besides the mention of Zones Three, Four and Five, there is a non-existent Zone Two symbolizing peace and orderliness. Zone Three, an area of peace and tranquillity is controlled by Queen Al-Ith. The barbaric Zones Four and Five are engaged in perpetual warfare. However, the curse of the Divine falls on Zone Three because its inhabitants are selfish. Consequently, Al-Ith has to embark on a process of purgation marrying the barbaric king of Zone four bearing him a son. Then the king marries the Queen of Zone Five in order to subdue her barbarity. Al-Ith, then, transcends to Zone two and her son becomes the joint ruler of Zones Three, Four and Five proclaiming hope and visualizing the theme of the novelist for cosmic unity.

Shikasta unfolds the fury of the probable Third World War in which inhabitants of the earth indulge in prolonged orgy of mutual destruction. Efforts for reconstruction and compromise fail due to partisan and sectarian attitudes. We are horrified at the aftermath of nuclear and chemical radiation. Out of necessity for form and modernity, the novel is a space fiction and, as such, stars, planets, galaxies abound the story. At the same time, it is obvious that the underlying theme revolves around the author's worry about degeneration of human life *enmasse*. Towards the close the reader succeeds in comprehending that Lessing recognizes the world as a part of the Cosmic Mind claiming that man continuously makes efforts to re-establish his relationship with the Divine Force. This idea is rooted in Sufi doctrine. The equivalent of a Sufi in this novel is symbolized by 'an elite group'. Thus, Lessing's view of life shifts her further to hope for resurrection of mankind after his eventual fall. Beginning from a paradisiacal world, the novelist's terrestrial history ends at the possible emergence of 'a golden age'. Her optimism, on one hand, makes her appear as a Christian and ideas of superior consciousness and the 'elite', on the other hand, indicate a perceptible tilt towards such an Asian mystic thought as Sufism.

The third novel of the series entitled *The Sirian Experiments* (1981) strengthens our belief in the Lessingian vision that man as microcosm must be subordinated to humanity at large which is the macrocosm. The recurring inference focuses on the idea that by developing superior consciousness we can crawl nearer to achieving commonweal. In this connection, Gerald Graff's theorization about postmodernism befits this novel:

> The quest for transcendence by way of a paradise within, not as an escape from outer reality, has become the focus of much contemporary cultural and artistic activity. An art and literature which celebrates the expansion of consciousness has established itself as an alternative to despair and resignation which mark the most austere forms of postmodernism.
>
> (*The Novel Today*, 238)

The first three novels of the series taken together certainly deserve to be recognized as a postmodern classic due to their mythical technique proving, at the same time, the endeavourance of the novelist for rewriting the history of human civilization.

The Making of the Representatives for Planet Eight (1983), the fourth novel in Canopus in Argos series portrays Johor, the Canopean agent and one of the "Providers" (Doris Lessing's terminology for the "Divine") in the process of saving the planets Shikasta and Sirius from extinction by imbibing in them the finer values of life. However, he faces a bigger challenge in protecting Planet Eight which is hounded by the threat of an ice age. This planet is ultimately submerged under ice but fifty chosen ones who had developed mental stability, superior consciousness and Sufi dervish-like grit and stoicism survive the crisis and are commissioned to rebuild their Planet renewing the upward progress of its civilization.

The last novel in the series, *The Sentimental Agents in the Volyen Empire* (1983) acclaimed by the critics as a "Social satire in the tradition of Voltaire and Swift" inclines to drift away from the Sufi mode of existence, the message ingrained in the narrative reflecting the idea that the life of extreme indulgence and pleasure is momentary, the series culminating in this way with the warning that evil is transient and its delectation is temporary whereas man is capable of rising higher and above the mire of vices by his superior mental power, a mutation as inducted in Sufi thought.

Lessing's attraction towards Sufism verges on the syllogism that this doctrine amalgamates the faith of the mystic communion with the Divine with the idea of total involvement in the general welfare of the community. Sufi principle excellently exemplifies the process of combining spirituality with humanism. Undoubtedly, Lessing resorted to writing due to her humanistic concern about the exploited Blacks and later adapted Sufism as her alter faith for personal tranquillity. In this sense, the novels that followed *Canopus in Argos* series are quite significant portraying characters who surrender their narrowcentric views for the sake of common good. Alice, the protagonist of the ironically titled novel, *The Good Terrorist* (1985) surrenders her militancy to work for the welfare of the society. In *The Fifth Child* (1988), Ben, a giant who has both biological colossusness and titanic mental strength, employs these faculties for helping others in spite of being mocked at as a freak. Lessing, later, wrote a sequel *Ben, in the World* (2000) with the purpose of developing the character of Ben taking him on a perpetual quest for meaning in life. Finally, he is accepted by the people and becomes instrumental in spreading the message of mutual tolerance. *The Sweetest Dream* (2001) embodies her concern for society once again. All her earlier themes find expression in this novel such as generation gap, romantic idealism, women liberation, holocaust of the world wars, disillusionment with Communism and her ultimate acceptance of Sufism.

A critical perusal of these novels of Doris Lessing substantiates that after her orientation to Sufism she contemplated seriously about the relationship between the individual and the collective—the microcosm and the macrocosm. She derived inspiration from Jafar Sadiq, a Sufi philosopher quoting him in her novel *A Ripple from the Storm* (1958) as follows:

> Man is the microcosm, creation the macrocosm—the unity...start with yourself, end with all. Before man, beyond man, transformation.

Doris Lessing was, evidently interested in the destiny of man because in an interview to Jonah Raskin she stated:

> What interests me more than anything is how our minds are changing, how our ways of perceiving reality are changing.
>
> (Schlueter, 66)

Unmistakably, Lessing is pointing towards the process of self-scrutiny which ultimately culminates in a quest for spiritual wholeness. Metaphorically concluding, the spiritual experiences of her protagonists may be equated with those mentioned in John Bunyan's *The Pilgrim's Progress* (1678) or even the evolution of T.S. Eliot's poetic theory. Eliot begins *The Waste Land* (1922) on a note of doubt and despair but the agony is finally resolved in *The Four Quartets* (1943). Similarly, in *The Golden Notebook* the novelist's denouement points to the attainment of self-emancipation through suffering, realization, purgation and ultimately resorting to mysticism. In the ensuing novels, she emphasizes that biological evolution is obsolete whereas mental evolution is the need of the time. Extracting cue from Sufism she mentions that telepathy and prophetic powers are a kind of spiritual attainment making a person self-purified thereby transcending the bounds of time and space. She firmly believed that mental and intellectual evolutions are capable of raising man's consciousness making the fusion of microcosm and macrocosm feasible.

A chronological study of Doris Lessing's novels enunciates the fact that she has been invariably concerned with the individual in its relationship to the collective. This fact maybe latent in her early novels but while composing *Landlocked* (1965) under the impact of Sufi thoughts, she began to manifest this relationship in broader terms, gradually concluding that the survival of humanity depends upon psychic mutation or a positive mental evolution. Her attitude towards the future of mankind is hopeful—that man is not destined to be doomed and can be saved. This vision is evident from her repeated use of the symbol of well-organized cities in various novels.

Doris Lessing has been perpetually aware that the forces of good and evil exist together and simultaneously in life. Evil endangers man's quest for happiness by suggesting short-cut measures consequently making man self-centred. His selfishness clashes with his conscience and his 'goal' is narrowed down to the attainment of his own 'interests', though apparently he fashions norms and institutions for the general good. The novelist severely condemns such a "societal convenience" (*The Memoirs of a Survivor*, 19) exhorting man to realize the basic goodness within him and spread around others the 'lasting happiness', which he can gain through the conscious process of psychic mutation. Lessing does not reject life but accepts it as the most precious gift of the Divine, hence desiring to save life.

Doris Lessing's diversion to Sufism culminated her quest. Eventually, she gave the message of mental and intellectual evolution which would raise the consciousness of man. As a consequence, the self would be completely effaced and all men would strive for the common good.

WORKS CITED

Bradbury, Malcolm. *The Novel Today: Contemporary Writers on Modern Fiction.* Manchester: Manchester University Press, 1977.

Bunyan, John. *The Pilgrim's Progress* (1678), London: Oxford University Press 1981 edn.

Dee Seligman, *Modern Fiction Studies*, "The Four-Faced Novelist", Vol. 26, No. 1, 1980.

Eliot, T.S. "The Waste Land" (1922), *Collected Poems 1909-1962.* London: Faber and Faber, 1963.

________. "The Four Quartets" (1943), *Collected Poems 1909-1962.* London: Faber and Faber, 1963.

Laing. R.D. *The Divided Self*, Middlesex: Penguin Books, 1965.

Lessing, Doris. *Walking in the Shade,* Volume *Two of My Autobiography, 1949-1962*. London and New York: HarperCollins, 1997.

________. *The Elephant in the Dark,* "An Ancient Way to New Freedom" (1972) (Ed) Leonard Lewin, New York: Dutton, 1976.

________. *Martha Quest* (1952), London: Granada rpt. 1958.

________. *The Four-Gated City* (1969), London: MacGibbon and Kee.

________. *A Ripple from the Storm* (1958), London: Granada rpt. 1977.

________. *Landlocked* (1965), London: Granada rpt. 1977.

________. *Briefing for a Descent into Hell* (1971), London: Granada rpt. 1977.

________. *The Summer before the Dark* (1973), New York: Bantam, rpt. 1974.

________. *The Memoirs of a Survivor* (1974), London: Octagen Press, 1974.

________. *Shikasta: Re: Colonised Planet 5* (1979), London: Jonathan Cape, 1979; New York: Knopf, 1979.

________. *Marriages Between Zones Three, Four and Five* (1980), London: Cape, 1980; New York: Knopf, 1980.

________. *The Sirian Experiments* (1981), London: Cape, 1981; New York: Knopf, 1981.

________. *The Making of the Representatives for Planet Eight* (1983), London: Cape, 1982; New York: Knopf, 1982.

________. *Documents Relating to the Sentimental Agents in the Volyen Empire* (1983), London: Cape, 1983; New York: Knopf, 1983.

________. *The Good Terrorist* (1985), London: Cape, 1985; New York: Knopf, 1985.

________. *The Fifth Child* (1988), London: Cape, 1988; New York: Knopf, 1988.

________. *Ben, in the World* (2000), London & New York: HarperCollins, 2000.

________. *The Sweetest Dream* (2001), London: Flamingo (HarperCollins), 2001; New York: HarperCollins, 2002.

Ralf Ellison's *Invisible Man*: A Southern Narrative

SHAHAJI V. GAIKWAD

SOUTHERN literature specifically refers to the literature of the American South. It is the literature written by the writers born in the region and who have a certain kind of attitude to life and a certain kind of subject matter to write on. The idea of Southern literature becomes clear by looking at its distinctive qualities which are added in making of it. H. Blair Rouse sees "Southern time and place" (126) as significant in Southern narrative and without which the idea of Southern literature is impossible. He adds that in Southern fiction the treatment of time is "a simple *statement* of the passage from one point of time to another, either in recorded history or in the lives of the fictional characters" (126). H. Blair Rouse elaborates his statement on time that "those novels and novelists which are most characteristically Southern, time as the essence of all that has happened in the...past becomes the factor of greatest importance in the fiction and may control the shaping of the narrative, the character development...the pattern of the work" (132). Writing about place Rouse says that "time and place are so closely involved, so integrated in their functions, as to be nearly indistinguishable" (135) in Southern narrative. Place is not just a sign indicating a location but does have real involvement in the structure and meaning of the work.

Charastically, Ralph Ellison's *Invisible Man* displays all the traits attributed to Southern narrative by H. Blair Rouse. Therefore, the present paper is an attempt to locate in the text of the fiction by Ellison the key attributes of Southern literature in order to establish it as a southern narrative. In the novel time past and the place turn out as the important factors that control both the nameless protagonist's development and the narrative too. The time past in the text is actually the nameless protagonist's Southern past embodied in the words of his dying grandfather—a half-mad war veteran—and the others are the words of the college president. In his deathbed the old man tells his grandson that the world is deceptive so that the boy must learn how to be deceptive. The old man spoke in elliptically paradoxes to express an ostensibly self-contradictory message. He insisted his family to follow his example and undermine the system while pretending to uphold it:

> 'Son, after I'm gone I want you to keep up the good fight. I never told you, but our life is a war and I have been a traitor all my born days, a spy in the enemy's country ever since I give up my gun back in Reconstruction. Live with your head in the lion's mouth. I want you to overcome 'em with yeses, undermine 'em with grins, agree 'em to death and destruction, let 'em swoller you till they vomit or bust wide open'. (Ellison 17)

These words have tremendous effect on the nameless protagonist however he is not sure what they mean. They become a "constant puzzle" (18) which always lay in the back of his mind. Throughout the narrative he tries to repress them there in the back of his mind, but they continually come up. These words are the nameless protagonist's Southern past which continually haunts him. He takes the old man's words as "a curse" and he thinks that if he follows them then he "would be lost" (18). He prefers humility which he thinks as the very essence of progress. But at the same time he cannot deny his past which gives him blackness.

The nameless protagonist's act of denying his past is denying his blackness—his Southern heritage embodied in his slave grandfather. His submission to the dehumanizing codes of white society through humility is an act of denying his heritage and accepting unquestionably the roles that white society assigns. He is caught in the dilemma and each of the episodes in the narrative shows his failure to use his sensibilities, his own power of discernment. He has lost the sense of his condition and he is equally unable to realize the objective of his search. Only when he reflects on his past while lying in the hole does he become aware of his own condition. He realizes that all his life people have been looking through him but unable to see him. It is because they have refused to see him and his blackness. In the PROLOGUE of the novel this nameless protagonist says that "I am invisible…simply because people refuse to see me" (7).

What he means here is that people refuse to see him as an individual as well as his humanity. In order to achieve his individual identity, the nameless protagonist turns to his Southern past and understands its meaning. He looks at his identity as a link in the chain of tradition. But this knowledge of self identity does not come to him till towards the end of the narrative. The earlier part of the narrative shows him with his idealism, ambition and expectation. He firmly believes then that without the white folks' approval he will be lost. His belief is exactly opposite of what his grandfather had said to him. The nameless protagonist fails to examine not only his grandfather's words but also the observable nature of the white folks' approval. The two parts of the narrative present his development from one stage to another stage. The first part, which takes place in the rural South, shows him at his defeat and his movement up north. The second part of the narrative shows the nameless protagonist angry and vindictive working as a spokesman of an organization. He has determined to undermine and destroy society.

In the South in a segregated school the nameless protagonist, along with other black boys, undergoes certain ordeals. He experiences the two acts: one, he watches the American flag wave on the undulating belly of a naked blond and the other, a battle royal and a scrabble for gold coins on an electrified rug. Each of the ordeals is designed for the black students' mockery yet the nameless protagonist hardly recognizes the disparity between his expectations and actual situation. He resents fighting in the royal battle not because the match itself is degrading, but because he is repelled by the notice of being lumped together with other black boys. He is devoted to the myth of racial uplift so that he desires to speak before the white citizens. He says that "I wanted to deliver my speech more than anything else in the world, because I felt that only these men could truly judge my ability" (25). The nameless protagonist identifies himself with white citizens but fails to understand his relationship with them.

His failure to understand the nature of his relationship with white citizens has the strong connection with his failure to understand the meaning of his grandfather's words. He takes the words as a "curse" denying the true meaning of them. The briefcase and the scholarship he receives for delivering a speech, the nameless protagonist takes them as his "triumph" (31) over his grandfather's "curse". He tries to cut himself off from the past and feels safe from it but this turns out as temporary feeling. The night following his receipt of scholarship and a briefcase, the nameless protagonist dreams of his grandfather who asks him to open the briefcase and read what is inside there. Obeying the old man the nameless protagonist reads as "Keep This Nigger Boy Running" (32). He comes out of the dream and wakes up only to listen to his grandfather laughing. However, he neglects it thinking that he cannot afford to understand the old man and takes his way to fulfill his aspirations.

In the State College for Negroes the nameless protagonist becomes further committed to the American dream. He and his fellow students virtually worship the administrators and trustees of the college as embodiments of the material success ensuing from hard work and clean living. They take Dr. Bledsoe as a visible image of what the students' best efforts may yield. They think that years of hard work make Dr. Bledsoe the president of the school and a prominent national leader. What the nameless protagonist and his fellow students don't know is that Dr. Bledsoe shares grandfather's belief in duplicity as a necessary precondition for achievement (Smith 28). But very soon the nameless protagonist comes to know that Dr. Bledsoe's 'legendry' humility is not genuine but just a performance; at the base he is manipulative, dishonest and opportunist. Dr. Bledsoe follows the old man's advice that the nameless protagonist has been neglecting.

The nameless protagonist sees second time that his grandfather's advice is followed by other black men. This time they are "field nigger" named Trueblood and a veteran—a former surgeon now in the local insane asylum. These two black men repeat the warning that the grandfather years before gave to the nameless protagonist. Trueblood presents himself an example of a black who accepts his past for a better life. The story of the field nigger is appalling because he impregnated his own daughter. He commits the act dreaming that he is in a white lady's bedroom. As he wakes, he finds himself mounted on his own daughter, Matty Lou. Next moments he is in a dilemma: How can he get away without sinning? He chooses to stay to sin since circumstance, Matty Lou and his own iron won't let him get away. Trueblood is cast out by his wife, Kate and community for committing incest with his daughter. He leaves for the wood to try to figure out if he is guilty or not.

In his attempts to prove him guiltless Trueblood consoles to think that a man can look at a little old pigtail girl and see her as a whore. His act is a sin but it came about in a dream. For a long time he tries to resolve the question whether he is guilty or not. In this strain Trueblood feels that his head is about to burst but he gets himself relieved from this situation by singing the blues. He tells that "All I know is *end up* singin' the blues, I sing me some blues that night ain't never been sang before..." (Ellison 58-59). The blues is Trueblood's heritage and singing of it gives him strength to overcome his guilt. He goes back to his daughter Matty Lou and his wife Kate and faces them. His returning home from exile is his act of refusing to believe white man's myth of guilt and pollution (Schor 61). On the other side, his singing of the blues is his accepting his heritage that helps him to overcome his past. Trueblood's identity is that he is a family man and, according to Schor, accepting family responsibility he gives his person manhood and meaning (61).

The nameless protagonist misses the essence of Trueblood's story; instead of taking it as a lesson, he is ashamed of it. He does not understand the fact that Trueblood survives only by accepting his past, his heritage. The nameless protagonist repeats his mistake in the veteran's case once again. He does not learn anything from the story of the veteran. The veteran tells the nameless protagonist, who is working as Norton's chauffeur, that he was graduated from the college on the hill and became a physician. He went to France during the world war to perform brain surgeries that won attention. When he returned, ten men in masks drove him out from a city at midnight while beating him with whips for saving a human life. The veteran thought then that being a doctor could bring dignity and other men health. He lived in France long enough to "forget some fundamentals…. Things about life. Such things as most peasants and folk people almost always know through experience" (78).

The veteran's story is taken at its surface by the nameless protagonist hence completely losing its essence. The veteran's behaviour towards the white men makes him worried, puts him in anxiety. The veteran acts towards the white men with a freedom which, the nameless protagonist thinks, may bring trouble. He still believes that not his heritage or his past or his people may help him to bring him success but the white patronage may. He continues to believe in the necessity of white patronage for success even after he expelled from the college by its self-seeking president. He views his expulsion from the college as from the Eden and he like the snake wriggling across the road as he is driven away. Ironically, the nameless protagonist is expelled for sin of obedience and not for using mother wit to tell a lie. Bledsoe once had asked him "You're black and living in the South—did you forget how to lie?" (116). In spite of the fact that Bledsoe himself is expert in masking and lying, not to follow him means to defect the ideals of the college.

The nameless protagonist accepts his banishment from the college as due to his own fault. He is unable to see the real snake in the garden. He retains his innocence, his belief in the myth of American dream and racial uplift while refusing the meaning of his southern heritage. He is unable to understand that his heritage may sharpen his senses and will help him to know his own situation. The talk of Norton demands from him to invest in the opportunities of the future "at the expense of the lessons of the past" (Smith 33). During his early days in New York City, the nameless protagonist is shown thinking of future and is reluctant to reflect on his past. In his room in the Men's House he puts aside the Bible because it makes him homesick and he has no time for nostalgia. He tells that "this made me homesick and I put the Bible aside. This was New York. I had to get a job and earn money" (Ellison 134). In the South, he was at home without feeling homesick. In the North, he is out of place and out of history too. This treatment of place and time is typical in the Southern narrative giving it a different identity.

Like place and time, the treatment of people adds a Southern flavour to the Southern narrative. On the way to a Mr. Emerson's office early in the morning the nameless protagonist hears a clear singing of blue notes. A cart man is singing it and surprisingly he recognizes the nameless protagonist. He claims his kinship with the nameless protagonist with a remark that "I know you from down home" (Ellison 141). The cart man walks along with the nameless protagonist while telling him that he does not need to put up appearances. The cart man displays his Southern identity for he knows that down South each one knows everyone. The nameless protagonist fails to learn from the cart man's singing but certainly it makes him homesick and, as a result, he seeks a certain comfort in the cart man's company. What the nameless protagonist fails to learn is that the cart man loves what is his and not what looks good. Southern acquaintance is a unique feature of Southern identity involving time, place and people. Ralf Ellison exploits all three in order to make his narrative a Southern narrative.

The narrative of *Invisible Man* reveals the nameless protagonist's inability to understand what is his. He is unable to decide what belongs to him. The blues belongs to him but he does not accept it as he does not accept the cart man so that he cannot find out its theme or subject to which it sings. His belongings can give him is identity and the purpose. He is recognizably a Southern boy but he persistently disowns his Southern heritage. The counterman recognizes him as a southern boy and suggests for him a special breakfast of pork chop and grits. At this the nameless protagonist wonders that "could everyone see that I was Southern?" (145). In order to hide his Southern identity he suppresses his hunger for pork chop and grits and orders for toast and juice. He tries to avoid whatever is Southern about him including his manner of speaking. He wants to refine in his taste rather than remaining just a "southern black." However very soon he comes out of this mentality; when he reads Bledsoe's letter he comes to know that refined taste will not necessarily get him anywhere.

The nameless protagonist is disillusioned of his ideas of success through refinement and for the first time he becomes less defensive against his past heritage. He tries to think about his past and learn from it instead of running from it. On the way home from Emerson's office he begins to hum the melody that someone near him whistled. The tune jars his memory but remind him of the song from his childhood. He reconstructs the song "O well they picked poor Robin clean" (158). He is able to understand the song's meaning and applies it to know his own situation. Earlier he has denied all knowledge that folksong and childhood songs do give to his community. But now he admits that they contain lessons that could be applied to his present life. The reading of the letter seven unleashes his wrath and he wants to kill Bledsoe. His determination to take revenge is the motive power of the second section of the book. He joins the revolutionary Brotherhood while losing his natural instinct.

The Brotherhood takes the interest of the individual as insignificant before the interest of the organization. The nameless protagonist is told in his first meeting that he must not waste his emotions on individuals because they don't count. The organization gives him a new name thus cutting him from his past and offering him absolute new beginning. He conforms to the Brotherhood's rules because, he thinks, it provides him with a system of belief that makes individual and political action significant. But joining the organization is yet another mistake that the nameless protagonist commits. His eagerness to escape the past and begin his life anew dooms him to repeat his earlier mistakes. He does not realize the fact that he is being mistreated by the Brotherhood. He trusts the Brotherhood so much that he takes his reprimanding by his superiors as a sign of their faith in the organization. But the sequence of events which culminates in Tod Clifton's murder precipitates him through re-examination of himself and his relation to authority and ideology. He realizes that the Brotherhood has ignored the interest of the race and that Clifton's Sambo dolls dangling on a string are metaphors of caricature of black members manipulated by the white leadership.

Clifton's death is seen by the Brotherhood spokesman as the murder of a traitor; an event that concerns the members minimally. When the nameless protagonist organizes a hero's funeral he is rebuked for it. He is as invisible in the organization as he was in his hometown and college. He has mistakenly thought that the Brotherhood would help him to find purpose and meaning of his life. He thinks that he should leave the organization but he can't bring himself to do so. He has no friend outside the organization so that he rules out possibility of any independent role. He decides that he would remain in the organization and tell them what they wanted to hear till the reality of Harlem explodes in their faces. This is the revenge he wants to take on the members of the organization and he will use his invisibility as a means. He would accept his past without any hesitation, "I began to accept my past and, as I accepted it, I felt memories welling up within me" (409), he says. He rejects the assumption that his past experiences are meaningless and merely sequences in favour of the belief that they make up who he is.

In his youth the nameless protagonist thought that the past was the best when put at a distance and that identity could be changed at will and defined by one's affiliations. But this was not true. As he writes the narrative he comes to know that all other imposed identities are false; the sum of one's experiences is one's true identity and to deny the past is to deny oneself:

> It was as though I'd learned suddenly to look around corners; images of past humiliations flickered through my head and I saw that they were more than separate experiences. They were me; they defined me. I was my experiences and my experiences were me, and no blind men, no matter how powerful they became, even if they conquered the world, could take that, or change one single itch, taunt, laugh, cry, scar, ache, rage or pain of it. (409)

The nameless protagonist accepts his past and defines his identity as a sum of his experiences. This is Southern treatment of past which gives the Southern character his identity. His identity is shaped and mould by his heritage and culture. Now he is ready to follow his grandfather's advice; he wants to test it though he is not sure what the words in it mean:

> I didn't know what my grandfather has meant but I was ready to test his advice. I'd overcome them with yeses and undermines them with grins. (409)

The nameless narrator-protagonist turns to his past-his grandfather's advice. The words of the old man haunt the grandson all his life but he tries to escape them. He cannot understand the significance of the old man's words because he is not interested in them. When he accepts his grandfather's advice as his heritage, he could understand the meaning of them. The old man's anger was directed against the condition that denied him his right to human dignity. His words claim the principle of commitment to equality and justice to all.

These words of a former slave make his grandson aware of his responsibility to defend his right. The grandson thinks that his grandfather's slavery was a social condition, and not a condition of mind (Schor 104). The nameless protagonist understands that the previous condition of servitude has given him a dual enriched heritage. In calling back the series of events leading to his present condition, he blames the outside world. But soon he realizes that he is equally responsible for it. He ran from what was his heritage and on occasions he even suppressed it. His ambition carried him to a slavish imitation of the whiteness that denied him his identity till he accepts his past and heritage. He was not invisible to them but to himself. He denied the fundamental reality, his race, the black that he is. Only after reviewing his experiences the nameless protagonist could give them shape and meaning. Ellison links the past with his hero's identity: refusal to accept the past leaves the hero invisible; acceptance of it gives him identity. Like other Southern writers Ellison looks at the past as a store of knowledge by which the hero can understand his present condition. He uses the past in *Invisible Man* to point where it controls the narrative and the character development. There is no doubt that in all respect this novel is a Southern narrative.

WORKS CITED

Ellison, Ralf. *Invisible Man*. England: Penguin Books, 1965.

Rouse, H. Blair. "Time and Place in Southern Fiction." *Southern Renascene*. Ed. Louis D. Rubin, Jr., and Jacob Robert D. Baltimore: The John Hopkins Press, 1953.

Schor, Edith. *Visible Ellison: A Study of Ralf Ellison's Fiction*. London: Greenwood Press, 1993.

Smith, Valerie. "The Meaning of Narration in Invisible Man." Ed. Robert O'Meally. *New Essays on Invisible Man*. Cambridge: Cambridge University Press, 1988.

Nature as Literary Construct: The Ironic Foregrounding of the Protagonist's Predicament in Anita Desai's *In Custody*

REENA MITRA

THE artistic intention of a novelist is seldom realized by a mere physical and topographical depiction of the milieu and the scenic backcloth to all that transpires in the work. What is of consequence to him is the creation of an honest and authentic environment that enables his characters to enact their lives in the most plausible way. In Thomas Hardy's novels, for instance, the characters and the places they inhabit are so heighten and underscore the emotional experiences of the individuals and offer a fictional canvas for all human behaviour to be scrutinized. The setting of these novels like Casterbridge in *The Mayor of Casterbridge* and Egdon Health in *The Return of the Native* are not just photographs in words but the immediate milieu of the respective protagonists, with whatever is marginal and incidental seemingly casually thrown in for effect. This makes us conscious of the actual unplanned layout of the intimate rural areas to which they belong and thus lends the background further authenticity.

The essentiality of the author's vision and his world view are reflected in the incidents of the novel—major and minor. With the social environment in life gaining centrality in the changing paradigms of existence in modern India, Anita Desai in *In Custody* reminds us of and draws our attention to the role of Nature in the lives of individuals. Her stance with regard to the background of her novel, *In Custody*, is singularly striking as the setting assumes a function far more integral to the explication of the plot than was customary in literary practice with her contemporaries. Thus, important here is the way in which she herself responds to Nature and makes her protagonist lusciously register and acknowledge it as fundamental to the human psyche and to what may be called the "mindscape" at any particular point of time in cognition. It becomes for her more specifically as Canon Cheyne puts it, "a magazine of symbols"[1] bearing upon human life. She is, in this particular novel selected for substantiation, inclined towards greater elaboration of the environmental moat around for the natural backdrop here becomes vital in its association with human events that provide the scaffolding; in fact, the growing significance of Nature sometimes tends to encroach upon the story itself, so that in view of the changing methods of narrative art, Nature become the structural principle which at times, ironically and cruelly, projects the protagonist's life with a sneer and at times again, exudes a sense of empathy that overtakes the earlier heedlessness and disregard. In the ultimate analysis, however, the entire range of Deven's emotions as they stage past in the novel, one overtaking the other in quick succession, are all distilled into descriptions of landscape and setting which are made to articulate the total experience of the central character, reeling under the "restrictive pressures...powerfully embodied in the seting."[2]

It is the multiplicity of minor incidents in the *In Custody* that offers the assurance of particularized reality and the veracity of the natural world. Insignificant events of plant, bird and animal life in Nature manifest the same grain of native reality, and yet, all the portending disaster of Deven's predicament—its loneliness and its desolate paltriness—is focused in the mirroring eyes of the birds and the animals around. There is the same sensitive sincerity to the depiction of minutiae and to the articulation of facts, the same intrinsic vision in rendering the solidity and specificity of experience in terms of aspects of Nature.

Though Nature in *In Custody* assumes the semblance of a metaphor, if scratched deeper, it is seen essentially to be a reality that one has to encounter in life to achieve anything or to get anywhere and it persistently acts in its own persuasive, precipitous, meaningful essentiality by thwarting human purposes and eventually by repressing any attempt at an assertion of self-esteem.

The dramatic motivation provided by Nature in *In Custody* is central to almost every aspect of the novel. It also controls the style giving it a substantial density of weave with symbolic intensity being stoically conveyed by the obvious and the apparent itself with unimpeded placidity maintaining the most intimate observation. Style here comprises not verbal quality alone, but an aspect of divination that blends with observation providing the driving force in the novel. Desai is able to use setting and atmosphere for a symbolic representation which though apparently blunt, maintains its naturalistic premise the exists as Final Cause, fully infused with dramatic inexorability, governing definitively, the actions and movements of the protagonist, Deven.

Nature as an all-pervasive element in deciding the course of individual life often assumes a dramatic significance that accords it an irreducible solidity in the larger perspective. The growth of a novelist is believed to be commensurate with his increasing ability to cultivate immediacy and tactility in his descriptions. It is when we confront the eternal framework of Nature in a literary construct that we become conscious of the overpowering and undilutable reality of the landscape, which either influences, even if it be in some remote way, the destinies of people or reflects the moods or the states of mind of the protagonist, and by doing so, reinforces the effect of those mental states and moods upon the reader.

Anita Desai, in her article, "Flight of Forms" elucidates the process of creative writing and explains how it is applicable to her own novels. The creative writer, she believes:

> ...writes without knowing why he writes. He writes the way a spider spins; it is all he knows how to do and he does it without thought, almost without consciousness. To him, it is a compulsive and instinctive act. I can think of a number of metaphors to illustrate this act; and it may be of significance that all that occur to me are drawn from nature.[3]

Desai uses evocative language in her descriptions of Nature. She endows words with an irresistible sensuous appeal and exults in the power of her eloquence. She depicts moods, conflicting choices and inner experiences and explores the inharmonious relationships of man springing from the incompatibility of partners in marriage—all with the help of richly suggestive nature imagery.

In Anita Desai's nature descriptions accurate observation and delicate poetic feelings are remarkably blended and stark facts are clad in striking imagery which harmonizes with the mood of the central character. For minute observation and vivid painting of details of natural scenery, Desai is almost unrivalled and often impresses us with microscopic effects. Few novelists have ever dealt with the minutiae of Nature as adeptly as she has. Her nature descriptions are characterized by an accuracy and delicacy of perception, beauty of delineation and felicity of translation into language of that which she perceives.

In Anita Desai's novels, right from her earliest one, *Cry, The Peacock* written in 1963, Nature is a powerful presence that dominates the scene of action and in its fabric are interwoven hope, despair, defeat and illusion. As she herself admits in an interview, the natural landscapes depicted in her novels are important to her—"The visual images and sounds, smells and textures of the places, I know are my material."[4] In *Cry, The Peacock*, the dance of peacocks itself is a blend of bliss and agony and reflects the mental state of Maya, the protagonist. In *Voices in the City*, Monisha's diary throws light on her love of nature. In *Bye-Bye, Blackbird*, too, Sarah's inner landscape is linked to the natural world around her. In *Where Shall We Go This Summer?,* Sita finds security in the lap nature. In *Fire on the Mountain*, the picturesque backdrop of Kasauli and its pine-scented hills provide a lavish fare of flora and fauna in a variety of forms. In *Clear Light of Day* the koel's call sets the tone of the novel.

In Custody is a novel that is distinctively different from all other novels of Anita Desai in that it is for the first time that a male character holds centre-stage in a work of hers and her treatment of Nature, too, is characterized here by a primarily ironic tone, a tone which intensifies as well as mocks at the misery born of the futility of human effort. This ambivalence in tone lends the narrative a compelling vigour and an added dimension.

In Custody, nominated for the 1984 Booker McConnell Prize, presents the antithesis between exaltation and mortification, between misperception and reality in the context of the plight of degenerate Urdu poetry in the contemporary era. Deven, with his inherent poetic sensibility exhibits a total lack of interest and concern in his profession as a lecturer of Hindi. His performance as a teacher reflects this indifference and ennui and he remains unappreciated and unrecognized by all who matter. His vain enthusiasm for Urdu poetry makes him fall prey to Murad's suggestion of his interviewing Nur Shajehanabadi, the famous Urdu poet, for an article in the Urdu magazine, *Awaz*. Lured by visions of name and fame Deven accepts the offer but soon his world of romantic illusions falls miserably apart for he finds Nur hardly measuring up to the poet he had visualized as his idol. Total disillusionment sets in when he actually meets "the man so clearly a hero,"[5] the great poet, the "superior being",[6] who is now no more than an old man engulfed by the intractable whirlpool of worldly reality, a total picture of debility and infirmity. This engulfment of Nur by the blasé world around is symbolically and effectively suggested by reference to the canal water turning "concentrically in a whirlpool."[7] The maelstrom, however, does not spare Deven either and he is encompassed by a sense of defeatism which with great determination he shakes off at the end to emerge as "the custodian of Nur's very soul and spirit."[8] Anita Desai very adeptly uses here nature as metaphor for calamities in life, and nature, again, as metaphor for emergence from these calamities.

Deven, like Monisha in *Voices in the City* and Maya in *Cry, The Peacock*, lives in a world of make-believe in which he imagines himself to be the sole custodian of Nur's poetry and feels that he should salvage it for posterity. It is this desire to assume the responsibility of preserving and perpetuating the Urdu couplets of Nur, now an inconceivably decadent poet, that worsens Deven's lot and makes him suffer undeservedly. As Jasbir Jain comments with regard to Anita Desai's novels "Roles become facades, they cloud the reality, they confine and blind and order the behaviour of the characters."[9]

The dramatic motivation (or demotivation?) provided by natural conditions is central to every aspect of *In Custody*. It defines the style of the novelist: page after page displays a wrought density of texture that emerges not from any specific verbal quality but from the actual motivational impact of the natural surroundings that often turn squalid to match the human low that plagues Deven when he is conscious of the shards of his shattered literary aspirations all around him. Symbolic depth in the novel is communicated by the physical surface of things with unhampered transparency as in the following lines:

> .... There was nothing to be heard but the water rushing past the banks.... He could slip in if he was not careful.[10]

On the other hand, the homeliest conviction of fact is convincingly preserved: "Dust lay heaped in smell piles around her."[11] All these together become aspects of Nature that assume almost dramatic causational necessity guiding the protagonist's course of action.

The natural environment in *In Custody* sets the tone of the novel to be dark and sombre, communicated to us as a symbol of Deven's inexorable circumstances that impede the realization of his literary ideals. So, Nature in this work is not a passive backdrop but an existence that intensifies and enhances the native proclivities of an individual struggling to survive with a modicum of dignity. The dilemma of Deven as to whether he should pursue his artistic yearnings or renounce them to provide the minimal comforts due to his wife and child is the dilemma of a morally individualizing consciousness in its earthy blend, a condition restraining man from soaring high in an imaginative and enterprising flight of fancy.

Dr. R.A. Singh, in his exhaustive study of the existential characters of Arun Joshi and Anita Desai, refers to five inter-related operational conditions which determine the plight of the modern man in a hostile world, namely, "powerlessness, normlessness, isolation, self-estrangement and meaninglessness."[12] All of these are fully operative in the life of Deven in *In Custody* and Nature seems to be in connivance with all these factors in threatening to corrode every sphere of life, in reducing him to dust, the word 'dust' in the text assuming multiple connotations.

McIntosh, in his elucidation of Shakespeare's use of "grammatical clues" to characters has endorsed "the widespread implication of every slight linguistic nuance", which is "capable of yielding its import to us."[13] Anita Desai, too, is fully conscious of the possibilities of the medium she has chosen to write in. Indepth studies and critical interpretations of her novels have strengthened the belief that

> ...an analysis of linguistic correlates of her characters' psychographs is most likely to reveal interesting correspondences between characters and the language used by them and *about them*. (italics mine)[14]

The language of *In Custody* is equally revelatory of the psyche of her protagonist, Deven, and of the problems that he encounters in the pursuit of his literary objectives. The imagery in the novel is in terms of dull, drab and subdued colours like black and grey. This is corroborated by expressions like "a grove of blackened acacian trees"[15] and "the grey clay."[16] These expressions suggest a stifling atmosphere everywhere.

In *In Custody*, too, as in Anita Desai's world of women in her other novels, we witness

> a world where the central harmony is aspired to but not arrived at, and the desire to love and live clashes—at times violently—with the desire to achieve harmony.[17]

Deven often finds himself on the verge of neurosis in trying to happily bring together his domestic world and the world of artistic aspirations. His efforts to create in his life "cosmos out of chaos,"[18] as N. Ramachandran Nair puts it, do bear fruit when he fortifies himself at the end to fight his battle alone:

> He had imagined he was taking Nur's poetry into safe custody, and not realized that if he was to be custodian of Nur's genius, then

> Nur would become his custodian and place him in custody too. This alliance could be considered an unendurable burden—or else a shining honour. Both demanded an equal strength.[19]

At the end, however, Deven proves equal to the situation and displays a rare kind of confidence and resolution born of physical and psychological agony. He decides unreservedly to be the guardian and trustee of Nur's poetry, come what may:

> He turned back. He walked up the path. Soon the Sun would be up and blazing. The day would begin with its calamities. They would flash out of the sky and cut him down like swords. He would run to meet them. He ran, stopping only to pull a branch of thorns from under his foot.[20]

Despite the fact that the male consciousness torn apart by acute psychological agony is not Desai's forte, she has communicated to us the agonies of the wounded self through powerful perceptions and engrossing nature descriptions doled out in a vibrant style. The primary mode of narration is largely dependent on the use of Nature as metaphor, nature as a symbol for the disastrous conditions of life. Deven, in his final run, after pulling out the thorns from under his foot, affirms the eventual assemblage of his shattered self into one who could confront life with equanimity and poise. He realizes the existence of the symbiotic relationship that prevails between Nur and himself. The canal water turning "concentrically in a whirlpool"[21] is a symbol for this convergence of his co-extensive attitudes towards Nur—his admiration for his poetry and his consciousness of the decadence that had set in—to arouse his stable self, which is now instilled with a new clarity and vision.

The novelist's depiction of Mirpore, like E.M. Forster's delineation of Chandrapore in *A Passage to India* is "a deliberate focused evocation—only more detailed and more heavily laced with irony."[22] The two lines which describe Mirpore in a nutshell are not without an inherent sense of irony: "…Although it lacked history, the town had probably existed for centuries in its most basic, most elemental form."[23]

What made this place "enduring" and never essentially inclined to change was the fact that

> …the dust beneath was always present, always perceptible. In fact, it managed to escape from under the asphalt and to rise and spread through the town, summer and winter, a constant presence, thick enough to be seen and felt. During the monsoon, always brief and

> disappointing on this northern plain, more than a thousand miles from the coast, it turned to mud. But the Sun came out again very soon and dried it to its usual grey and granular form. The citizens of Mirpore, petty tradesmen rather than agriculturists, could not be blamed for failing to understand those patriotic songs and slogans about the soil, the earth. To them it was so palpably dust.[24]

Dust thus becomes the predominant imagery in the novel. No resident of the place can ever escape "the ubiquitous dust of Mirpore."[25] This overwhelming consciousness of the presence of dust in everything associated with Mirpore emanates from what R.K. Gupta identifies as "the clear unambiguous images of this novel which are precise in their visual quality."[26]

The novel thus proceeds with the help of images, metaphors and symbols, most of which draw from the world of Nature. There is an abundance of colour imagery but the colours are almost always toned down or given a negative connotation by the use of epithets that detract from the normal vibrant colour. We have, in the novel, expressions like "acid-green" "pale-yellow", "withered and grey", "yellowed foliage", "pale-flash", "yellow-grey sky", "flattened grey world", "spittle-flecked red lips"—all suggestive of a kind of blight that seems to have struck them. This, perhaps, is in conformity with the protagonist's state of mind.

Bird and animal images in the text of the novel relate, almost invariably, to the central character's despair and suffering and foreground the "greyness" in his life. The sight of the dead stray dog, when on his way to Delhi, unnerves Deven as he sees prefigured in it his own prospective predicament. The reference to crows alighting on the dead dog connotes prey-predator images suggestive of Deven's situation in life where he is always cast in the role of the hunted. There are multiple references to Deven imagining himself to be "like a caged animal in a zoo" or "a trapped animal."[27]

The image of the pet pigeons of Nur turns from being "a symbol of flight and song"[28] into an impending threat to the very spring of poetry in him:

> My pigeons are dying…when the last of my pigeons is gone, I will cease to write poetry forever. I will go with them.[29]

In another bird image in the novel, the parrot symbolizes a rare moment of joy and pleasure in an unexciting and drab stretch of life—"one brilliant feather of spring green fluttered down through the air and fell at their feet in the grey clay."[30]

Nature in *In Custody* is again symbolized by the 'neem' tree growing outside the wall of the courtyard of Deven's house. Because of its "yellowed-foliage" it does not provide much shade; rather, it is a liability that obstructs the passage of fresh air: "No message came whispering on a nocturnal breeze; every leaf on the neem tree hung stiff, lifeless."[31]

The most characteristic feature of the countenance of Mirpore is its dryness and aridity, suggestive of infertility. Mirpore, we are told at the very outset, "spared no effort to give an impression of total aridity."[32] The town lacked a river and their stood in the shabby municipal park "an empty fountain painted blue."[33] In brief, we are given an inescapable impression of "Mirpore's addiction to total dehydration."[34] All this is clearly suggestive of the desolation in the monotonous life that Deven was almost compelled to live in Mirpore. His flights to give form to his immense literary yearnings are always impeded by the grim realities of the demands made on him as husband, father and lecturer.

Malashri Lal, in her essay on "Multilocality: International Themes in Women's Short Stories in English", categorically states that "Anita Desai's world is imbued...with psychological density."[35] This is said of her short stories but is equally true of her novels. The density of the mind referred to is as stated earlier, communicated to us through a profuse use of Nature which reinforces her depiction of the life and character of her protagonist, Deven. Imperceptibly the novelist blends external nature and human life together in the couplet she quotes as a composition of Nur coming to Deven's mind: "Night ends, dawn breaks, and sorrow reappears Addressing us in morning light, with a cock's shrill crow."[36] Rarely did a morning scene appear to be positively idyllic, and when it did, the idyll was soon demolished.

Anita Desai's novels, then, are clear expositions of her belief in the correspondence between the inner landscape of a character and his external environment. As in Tennyson's poetry, in her novels, too, Nature is subordinated to the varying moods of man and presented from the human standpoint. Desai has the rare power of giving atmosphere to a novel, of suggesting correspondence and interaction between the mind and its surroundings, between the situation and the subjective stance, at the time of a crisis in life. Nature, to her, though it appears to be dominant, is essentially a mirror that reflects human sentiments. Sorrow and disillusionment, in varying degrees of poignancy and cognition provide her the inspiration for some of the most absorbing scenes in *In Custody*.

K.R.S. Iyengar, in his assessment of Anita Desai's novels, states that:

> …the inner climate, the climate of sensibility that lours or clears or rumbles like thunder or suddenly blazes like lightning, is more compelling than the outer weather, the physical geography or the visible action.[37]

Yet "the outer weather" certainly does reinforce the experiences of exhilaration or desperation as experienced by the protagonist. Nature seems to observe and reverberate the vacillations of human emotions that are recorded on the sensibility graph.

NOTES

1. Cited in W.H. Hudson, "On the Treatment of Nature in Poetry". *An Introduction to the Study of Literature.* London: Harrap and Co., 1910, rpt. 1963. 323.
2. John Press, ed., *Commonwealth Literature* published in 1965, extracts from the proceedings of a Conference held at Bodington Hall, organized by the University of Leeds, 9-12 Sept., 1964.
3. Anita Desai, "Flight of Forms". India International Centre Quarterly, Vol. 10, Number 4, 1983.
4. Sheth, Kataki's interview with Anita Desai. *Imprint.* June, 1984.
5. Anita Desai, *In Custody.* New Delhi: Penguin Books, 1984, rpt. 1999, 39.
6. *Ibid.*, 38.
7. *Ibid.*, 204.
8. *Ibid.*
9. Jasbir Jain, *Stairs to the Attic: The Novels of Anita Desai.* Jaipur: Printwell, 1987, 134.
10. *In Custody*, 202.
11. *Ibid.*, 193.
12. R.A. Singh, *Existential Characters of Arun Joshi and Anita Desai.* Bareilly: Prakash Book Depot, 1991, 81.
13. Angus McIntosh, "'As You Like It': A Grammatical Clue to Character". *A Review of English Literature.* 4/2, 1963.
14. R.S. Pathak, "Anita Desai's Fiction: Character, Semantic Space and Linguistic Correlates". *Modern Indian Novel in English.* New Delhi: Creative Books, 1999. 95.

15. *In Custody*, 64.
16. *Ibid.*, 73.
17. Jasbir Jain, "Anita Desai". *Indian English Novelists: An Anthology of Critical Essays.* ed. Madhusudan Prasad. New Delhi: Sterling, 1982, 23.
18. Ramachandran Nair, "'*In Custody*': The Road Not Taken". *Indian Women Novelists.* Vol. 4. ed. R.K. Dhawan. New Delhi: Prestige Books, 1991, 94.
19. *In Custody*, 203.
20. *Ibid.*, 204.
21. *Ibid.*
22. Viney Kripal, "An Image of India: A Study of Anita Desai's *In Custody*. ARIEL: A Review of International English Literature, 1984. ariel ucalgary. ca.
23. *In Custody*. 19.
24. *Ibid.*, 20.
25. *Ibid.*
26. R.K. Gupta, *The Novels of Anita Desai: A Feminist Perspective.* New Delhi: Atlantic Publishers and Distributors, 2002, 134.
27. *In Custody*. 131.
28. *Ibid.*, 48.
29. *Ibid.*, 200.
30. *Ibid.*, 73.
31. *Ibid.*, 131.
32. *Ibid.*, 21.
33. *Ibid.*, 22.
34. *Ibid.*
35. Malashri Lal, "Multilocality: International Themes in Women's Short Stories in English". *Signifying the Self.* ed. Malashri Lal, Shormishtha Panja and Sumanyu Satpathy, New Delhi: Macmillan India Ltd., 2004, 157.
36. *In Custody*, 65.
37. K.R. Srinivasa Iyengar, "A Note on Anita Desai's Novels". *The Banasthali Patrika.* ed. Rameshwar Gupta, January, 1969, No. 12. 64.

'The Existential Vision' in Anita Desai's *Fire on the Mountain*

BINOD KUMAR ROY

"EXISTENTIALISM gained permanence in the literary circle in the twentieth century. It is not really a "philosophy" in the traditional sense of the term, but it is a mode of thinking, a tendency or an attitude of a philosophical nature which manifested itself after the First World War. Soon afterwards, it spread in European countries and towards the end of the World War II, it became very influential in the academic circles and became a popular subject in social discussions," remarks Sinha (Sinha, 2007, 138). Sinha further elaborates, "Existentialism, is really a revival of thought of Soren Kierkegaard, the Danish writer who derived the doctrine of existentialism, when he realised that "the individual must be saved as individual," saved from religious systems, the industrial and technological age, the forces of nature that treat man merely as an object of scientific interest. Along with Kierkegaard, Nietzsche and Dostoevsky, through fictional and literary contributions, voiced their deep concern about man's condition. In the present age, scientific and technological advancements have reduced the individual to insignificant proportions in the industrial setup and consequently crushed all his private values" (Sinha, 2007, 138). Thus, we can say that existentialism is a philosophical movement which emphasizes on individual existence, freedom, and choice.

Man's existential anguish, a recurrent issue in literature, finds powerful representation in Indian English Fiction which presents sensitive individuals pitted against ontological realities. The novels by the Indian writers tend to explore the dilemmas and quests of the modern man trapped in a materialistic civilization which brings out his worst instincts and alienates him completely: "Subject to the importunities and anxieties of a fragile universe, devoid of the spontaneity of interpersonal sociability, and malignantly self-absorbed, the characters exemplify the ubiquitous predicament of the modern man" (Clement, 1995, 204).

Indian fiction in English, down the decades, has sought to capture the inner turmoil of the Indian psyche during the prolonged period of transition from the colonial times to the epochs of modernity. The conflicts that exist within one lead to a divide within oneself, that is "the hardest to bridge; the hardest to accept, to live with" (Deshpande, 1992, 201). The psycho-spiritual conflicts raise existential questions involving a sense of loss of identity, rootlessness, alienation and agnostic ambivalence, which can result in an acute sense of isolation.

Unlike most of the modern writers who misconstrue man's true condition by accepting bitterness about absurd existence, Anita Desai holds the view that the writer must continually struggle for the true depiction of man's condition and the mystery about it. During the execution of her process of exploration of this mystery, Anita Desai presents a fresh approach to reality, holds life as sacred asset and seeks to depict its richness, power and mystery through ideas that contradict the formidable stances of alienation and absurdity. Her characters "are usually sensitive women who, haunted by a peculiar sense of doom, withdraw into a sequestered world of their own" (Sharma, 1981, 166).

Shastri's comments in this context seem very relevant—"Anita Desai's novels are, by and large, concerned with the problem of finding a still centre from which the inevitable conflicts and contradictions of life are resolved" (Shastri, 1989, 101). Further, Nair rightly remarks, "Deeper psychological implications of human existence have ever been the prime concern of Anita Desai, the authentic cartographer of the inward terrain" (Nair, 1991, 78). Desai's forte is an exploration of sensibilities under stress and her familiar preoccupation with the problems of human psyche makes the ordeal of consciousness the aesthetic centre of her fiction. As Patil states—"In Anita Desai's novels, the inner workings, the inner sensibilities are more compelling than the outer weather, or the visible action" (Patil, 1991, 47). Desai delineates the inner lives of individuals who are in the throes of an existential crisis resulting from a sense of insecurity and a desperate need to belong. She portrays their inner struggle to maintain their individuality while finding some means of relating to the society also. Talking of her characters Solanki says—"Almost all of them are torn apart between attachment and alienation, between the desire to live and the wish to die; between a need for recognition and the self-effacement drives, and between an attempt to say 'no' to the reality of life but striving hard to find the method and means to live it" (Solanki, 1992, 22). Thus as a novelist, Anita Desai exhibits a strong proclivity towards the existentialist interpretation of the human predicament. In particular, she voices "the mute miseries and helplessness of married women tormented by existentialist problems and predicaments" (Prasad, 1981, 139). Sashi Paul in her article titled *Alienation to Existentialism: A Study of Anita Desai's Novels,* states, "Desai's protagonists are highly sensitive and terribly bewildered by the burden of living helplessly in the society with absurd realities. Therefore, her fictional world is full of imperfection and unfulfilment, hankering and helplessness, agony and anger, struggle and surrender. She is essentially a novelist of existential concerns" (Misra, 2001, 96-97).

Desai's novels from *Cry, The Peacock* to *Journey to Ithaca* are a study in the depth and persistence of human affliction, inexorably sensitive and loving and compassionate as her protagonists are Desai adds a new dimension to the genre of Indian fiction in English by probing the unquestionable existentialist concerns of her protagonists. Toeing the line of the existential humanists, to Desai, existentialism means "the mad or bad...the shocking, the sordid or the obscene" (Greene, 1950, 1).

Of all her novels, *Fire on the Mountain* has been considered as "the lyrical fictionalization of the quintessence of existentialism" (Gupta, 1984, 185). A close study of the texture and theme of the novel in relation to the tenets of existentialism justifies the above observation. It has been noted that "*Fire on the Mountain* displays skillful dramatization of experiences of certain women embroiled by the cross way of life" (Choudhary, 1995, 77). This novel discloses the existential angst experienced by the female protagonist Nanda Kaul, an old lady living in isolation and also projects the inner turmoil of a small girl, Raka, who is haunted by a sense of futility. Thirdly, it presents the plight of a helpless woman, Ila Das who is in conflict with forces that are too powerful to be encountered, resulting in her tragic death. Thus, the existential themes of solitude, alienation, the futility of human existence and struggle for survival constitute the major themes of the novel.

Fire on the Mountain comprises of three sections which are further divided into several short chapters of unequal length. The first section, "Nanda Kaul at Carignano" contains ten chapters and deals with the lonely life of Nanda Kaul, the main protagonist in Kasauli. The second section, "Raka Comes to Carignano" contains twenty-one chapters and depicts Nanda Kaul's change of attitude towards Raka, her great granddaughter. The third section, "Ila Das Leaves Carignano" contains thirteen chapters and presents the tragic end of Ila Das, Nanda Kaul's childhood friend.

In this novel, "the story element is very thin and there is practically no action except for the tragic end" (Indira, 1994, 96). The story moves round the inner lives of the two female protagonists, Nanda Kaul and Raka. Nanda Kaul is the wife of Mr. Kaul, the Vice Chancellor of the Punjab University. As the novel opens, Nanda Kaul is shown living in Carignano, far from the madding crowd leading a life of isolation and introspection. She avoids all human company and even the postman's arrival seems an intrusion to her. However, this quietude does not last long. Raka arrives at Carignano to convalesce after her typhoid attack. The old woman and the young girl live in double singleness. But as days pass by, Nanda Kaul unexpectedly finds herself drawn towards Raka. However, the little girl refuses to be befriended and escapes into the hills looking for company in solitude. Ila Das, Nanda Kaul's childhood friend visits Carignano to meet Raka. A onetime lecture in the Punjab University, Ila Das had lost her job subsequent to Mr. Kaul's retirement. She has come to Kasauli now in her new capacity as an officer in the social welfare department. She advocates against child marriage by enlightening the local people about the evils of this practice and earns the wrath of many of the villagers of whom Preet Singh is one. His efforts to barter his little daughter for a small chunk of land and a few goats have been successfully thwarted by Ila Das. He keeps looking for an opportunity to settle his score with her. One evening, when Ila Das returns late from Carignano to her humble house in the valleys, he waylays her, rapes and murders her. When the news of Ila Das's death reaches Nanda Kaul over the phone, she is rudely shocked and falls dead. Raka unaware of her great grandmother's death rushes into the house proclaiming wildly that she has set the forest on fire.

Nanda Kaul, Raka and to some extent Ila Das, are embodiments of the existential predicament experienced by the individual in an un-understanding and even hostile universe. A detailed examination of the characters of these protagonists brings to light how Anita Desai has succeeded in giving expression to her existentialist world-view through these characters and by a subtle use of imagery and symbols. When the novel begins, Nanda Kaul is presented as a recluse. Living all alone, except for the company of the servants who dare not disturb her privacy, she brooks no human presence. "She wanted no one and nothing else.

Whatever else came, or happened here, would be unwelcome intrusion and distraction" (3). She spends her days in isolation, musing about her past and experiencing the existential ennui. "From the musings of her agitated mind it appears that as the wife of the vice chancellor for the Punjab University and the mother of several children, she has lived a very busy and tiring life" (Raizada, 1984, 44). Anita Desai unfurls her past in the form of long interior monologues punctuated by authorial interruptions; Nanda Kaul had witnessed only betrayals and demands in life before her retirement to Kasauli. She had lived a monotonous life receiving and treating the endless stream of visitors who used to call on her vice-chancellor husband. Her husband had carried on a life-long affair with his mathematics mistress Miss David, whom he would have married, had she not been a Christian. Again, the memories of her children make Nanda Kaul shudder at the very thought of her past. As a mother of several children, all demanding and unaccommodative, she had been given too many anxious moments. Now all alone in Carignano, a house associated with many weird stories, Nanda Kaul feels that loneliness is the only essential condition of human life. Whenever she looks at the tall pine trees that stand out from among the underwood, she is reminded of her own alienation. Not exactly conscious of what she is waiting for, nonetheless, she is awaiting the inevitable end to all human existence: death. She is haunted by the existential angst which has led her to conclude that human life is basically a lonely struggle against the odds of life. In her case the odds have manifested themselves in the form of an adulterous husband and cantankerous children. Strongly convinced that life and dealt a raw deal to her, she has resolved to find the meaning, if any, of her existence in isolation. "She treasures her freedom, her privacy, glad her responsibilities towards her family are over, glad she needs nobody and nobody now needs her" (Krishnaswamy, 1983, 260). This has coloured her outlook on life to a large extent. Her reaction to the arrival of the postman and Raka, her invalid great granddaughter, makes it appear that she has become a misanthrope. But the truth seems to be that she is a sensitive person preoccupied with the real nature of her existence as opposed to the illusory life of her past as a vice-chancellor's wife and mother to children. "If Nanda Kaul was a recluse out of vengeance for a long life of duty and obligation, her great granddaughter was a recluse by nature, by instinct. She had not arrived at this condition by a long route of rejection and sacrifice (like Nanda Kaul) she was born to it, simply" (48). Desai's above observation about Raka's character at once brings out the similarity and difference with that of Nanda Kaul's in their mental makeup. Raka's character has been introduced by the novelist as a foil to Nanda Kaul's.

If Nanda Kaul symbolizes a particular aspect of existentialism, which is examined elsewhere in this chapter, Raka epitomizes another aspect of the existential predicament: the influence of her parents on her life. Anita Desai makes Raka both young temperamentally and solitude-loving. When Raka is first introduced, the reader is informed that she is the granddaughter of Asha, the most problematic of Nanda Kaul's daughters. That she is an unwelcome intruder into Nanda Kaul's life is suggested by an image. As Nanda Kaul first looks at her great grand daughter who is walking towards her, she reminds the old lady of an insect: "Raka slowed down, dragged her foot, and then came towards her great grandmother with something despairing in her attitude. She turned a pair of extravagantly large and somewhat bulging eyes about in a way that made the old lady feel more than ever her resemblance to an insect" (39). However, the old lady is shocked to see the pale and gaunt little girl and is moved to pity. But "to Nanda Kaul she was still an intruder, an outsider, a mosquito flown up from the plains to tease and worry" (40). Raka herself does not bother much about the "blatant lack of warmth" (40) exhibited by her great grandmother. She prefers to stay away from company. Like a wild animal newly caged, she keeps prowling barefoot in her room, looking at the stone heaps. She is not interested in flowers or playing as children of her age normally tend to do. By using two reptile images successively in a span of two pages, and by a suggestive hint about Raka's lack of interest in play and flowers, Desai impliedly establishes that there is something weird about her. Soon through several interior monologues enacted in Raka's subconscious mind, the reason for the abnormality in her is unfolded. The daughter of an ill-matched couple, Raka has been witness to the brutality and futility of human existence. She is haunted by the recollections of the nightmarish nights that have made her almost a child-stoic. Somewhere behind them, behind it all was her father, home from a party, stumbling and crashing through the curtains of the night, his mouth opening to let out a flood of rotten stench, beating at her mother with hammers and fists of abuse-harsh, filthy abuse that made Raka cower under her bedclothes and wet her mattress in fright, feeling the stream of urine warm and weakening between her legs like a stream of blood, and her mother lay down on the floor and shut her eyes and wept. Under her feet, in the dark, Raka felt that flat, wet jelly of her mother's being squelching and quivering, so that she didn't know where to put her feet and wept as she tried to get free of it. Ahead of her, no longer on the ground but at some distance now, her mother was crying. Then it was a jackal crying (72). The sudden shift from the interior monologue about her bitter past to the present observation of the jackal crying, the latter superimposed on the former brings out Raka's predicament. By doing this, the novelist likens the haunting memories to the crying jackals. So Raka's life is a close encounter with things that are wild and frightful—be it the memories of her mother beaten to pulp by a drunkard father or the chilling cry of the jackals. Instead of trying to escape from this harsh and unnerving experiences and memories, Raka goes farther and deeper into them as if to fathom the bottom of such wild realities. After some initial hesitation, she ventures deep down the ravine to the Monkey Point—a place not frequented by others and from where the cries of the jackals are heard: "No one ever came here but Raka and the cuckoos that sand invisibly. These (the cuckoos) were not the dutiful domestic birds that called Nanda Kaul to attention at Carignano. They were the demented birds that raved and beckoned Raka on to a land where there was no sound, only silence, no light, only shade, and skeletons kept in beds of ash on which the footprints of jackals flowered in gray" (90). This passage effectively conveys Raka's plight and significance. She is at once a little girl with a splintered psyche and an unmistakable symbol of the individual's quest for meaning. The jackals are symbols of the mystery of life and Raka's walk to the Monkey Point is symbolic of her search for something unknown, yet inevitable and indispensable. Not all children would dare to brave the rough terrains of the ravines and impending menace of the jackals. Similarly, not all human beings are conscious of the futility of human existence nor are they in search of newer values. The existential theme of quest for meaning undertaken by those who refuse to remain merely as members of the multitude is well brought out in the lonely and mystified wanderings of Raka. In this respect, it has been pointed out by Shantha Krishnaswamy: "Her (Raka's) childhood has hardened her into a little core of solitary self-sufficiency and now, a young girl up here in the mountains...her spirit is defiant enough to go chanting 'I don't care, I don't care, I can't care of anything" (73). The conventional sweet smells and sounds of girlhood are ignored, she feels drawn by scenes of devastation and failure. The forest fires tingle her and she bursts from the shell of Carignano like a sharp, keen edged explosive to set fire to the mountainside (Krishnaswamy, 1983, 261-62).

The concluding part of the foregoing observation concerning Raka's predilection for the forest fires needs elaborate analysis for it has symbolic overtones. Ever since her arrival at Carignano, Raka evinces a keen interest in wild fire. This obsession with the forest fire provides yet another dimension with the forest fire provides to her existentialist preoccupations. Immediately after her arrival at Carignano, on witnessing a fire in the forest she becomes obsessed with forest fires for they seem to her the empirical manifestation of her inner conflict: whether to continue with her mediocre and painful and aimless existence imposed upon her by heredity and environment or to revolt against their dictates and attempt to create her own values. By an elaborate expression of her free will and demonstration of her ability to choose and act, she sets the forest on fire towards the end of the novel. The fire created by her is the result and manifestation of her existential angst to destroy the old and meaningless to make room for the new and significant. It is an affirmation of her search for values in an otherwise futile existence. Ila Das is the third female protagonist of the novel. Unlike Nanda Kaul and Raka who are central to the story, her role is only marginal. Nonetheless, Anita Desai has projected yet another aspect of the existentialist philosophy through her character. "Her life suggests another dimension of misery and meaningless existence" (Jena, 1989, 30). She is first introduced to the readers, when she calls Nanda Kaul on the phone and informs her of her intended visit to Kasauli to meet Raka. She speaks in a "hideous voice" (21) and is rather plain in her looks. Through a long interior monologue in Nanda Kaul's mind, the readers are informed of her past. She was Nanda Kaul's childhood friend. She had also served in the university as a lecturer, thanks to Nanda Kaul's good offices. But soon after the death of Mr. Kaul she had been ousted and had struggled a lot before finding the present employment as a social welfare officer. This lands her in an unenviable situation. She finds herself fighting a lonely battle against a mindless multitude. But she is not cowed down by adversity. She remains steadfast in her conviction and refuses to make any compromises. Though she is aware of the dire consequences that she might be forced to encounter, she remains faithful to her cause. She succeeds in stooping several such child-marriages, the prominent one being the marriage of Preet Singh's seven year old daughter. Sustaining herself on a meagre pay and putting up with the inevitable condition of loneliness, she wages a valiant battle against the dictates of the society. Finally, she pays a dear price for her convictions and refusal to compromise. She is raped and murdered by Preet Singh who has been dying for revenge. Though Ila Das plays a minor role in the novel, she is also an allegorical figure. She not only lives in isolation but also braves the brute majority with conviction and commitment as her tools. True, she meets with a tragic end but has made her existence significant in exhibiting courage and determination in the face of stiff resistance and threat to life. "Her real involvement in people's welfare assumes tremendous symbolic significance" (Jena, 1989, 30). She epitomises the existentialist concept of struggle against the odds of life. "For the existentialist, man is never just part of the cosmos but always stands to it in a relationship of tension with possibilities of tragic conflict" (Macquarrie, 1972, 17). She stands for the thinking individual who dares to exercise her free will and act according to her choice rather than submit meekly to the odds of life. The mindless tribal society in general and Preet Singh in particular, represent the malevolent aspect to human existence-forces that are bent upon thwarting the individual's purpose and undoing her. "One of the many ways of defining tragedy sees it as a clash between the aspiration of human freedom and creativity with a cosmic order that is stronger and defeats man" (Macquarrie, 1972, 17). Though Ila Das loses her chastity and life in the process of her struggle with such brute forces, her life has nonetheless become meaningful by virtue of the fact that she chooses a cause, fights for it and sacrifices herself in trying to accomplish her task. An examination of the use of symbolism and imagery in the novel proves beyond doubt the novelist's existential concern. She portrays a tragic world where no compromises are made, no epiphanies are exploded, to be totally destroyed, as the sensitive, the visionary suffer nothing but suffocation and oppression. So, the content of the novel is sheer violence. The lives of the principal characters are 'unloved' and 'unlived'.

In keeping with this concept, Anita Desai resorts to the effective employment of imagery and symbolism in *Fire on the Mountain*. For example, when she receives a call from Ila Das, Nanda Kaul "turned her head this way and that in an escape. She watched the white hen drag out a worm inch by resisting inch from the ground till it snapped in two. She felt like the worm herself, she winced at its mutilation" (21). The same is continued in the next page also: "Still starting at the hen which was greedily gulping down bits of worm, she thought of her husband's face and the way he would plait his fingers across his stomach..." (22). This prey-predator image of hen pecking at a worm is suggestive of Nanda Kaul's present inner turmoil. Another important image employed recurrently is that of the pine tree that stands burnt and alone, which is often an object of attraction for Nanda Kaul: "She was grey, tall and thin...she fancied she could merge with the pine tree and be mistaken for one. To be a tree, no more and no less, was prepared to undertake" (4). Again, this image also contributes to the existentialist theme of the novel. "Nanda's sense of identification with the pine trees suggests her desire for absolute stillness and withdrawal from life" (Indira, 1994, 97). The image of the charred pine tree is repeatedly employed in the novel. Raka is reminded of the futility of existence while she looks at the lonely hills and charred pine trees: "This hill, with its one destroyed house and one unbuilt one, on the ridge under the fire-singed pines, appealed to Raka.... There was something about it—illegitimate, uncompromising and lawless.... The sense of devastation and failure drew her, inspired her" (90). Images of insects like lizards, birds like eagles and parrots, and "the thematic image of the 'fire' with its connotations of violence and urgency occur at regular intervals, warning the reader of the impending tragedy" (Indira, 1994, 96).

Thus, the characters of Nanda Kaul, Raka and Ila Das are studies of women in isolation. Essentially a writer of existential inclinations, Anita Desai examines three important aspects of this school of thought through her protagonists. The predominant traits of existentialism are alienation, quest and conflict. These three aspects are epitomised in the lives of three female protagonists. Nanda Kaul is a study in alienation and existential angst. Raka symbolises the individual's quest for meaning in an otherwise futile life. Ila Das stands for the eternal conflict enacted in the human drama between the individual and the forces of determinism. One common ground for these three characters is that they are women who live in isolation both out if choice and compulsion. Desai has examined the predicament of women in wilderness by placing these three characters Kasauli, a place surrounded by hills and valleys, for removed from civilisation. She has consciously done it to examine the predicament and psyche of women in isolation. By placing her female protagonists with nature herself as the backdrop, Anita Desai has endowed a symbolic and universal significance to the plight of her protagonists. In this regard it has been pointed out: Essentially, Desai is a novelist of existentialist concerns, chiefly considering what F.H. Heinemann described as 'the enduring human condition.' In her novels, she has ably dwelt upon such existentialist themes as maladjustment, alienation, absurdity of human existence, quest for the ultimate meaning in life, decision, detachment, isolation and time as the fourth dimension, focusing on how women in the contemporary urban milieu are bravely struggling against or helplessly submitting to the relentless forces of absurd life (Prasad, 1984, 140).

Thus, we can conclude that, Desai has won a niche by exploring the emotional world of women, bringing to light the various deeper forces at work in feminine sensibility as well as psychology. This predilection leads her to examine the psyche of her women protagonists when they are confronted with the absurdity of life. This draws her attention to the darker side of life. She projects a tragic vision in her novels by placing her female protagonists in hostile situations. Desai further examines her women protagonists as individuals who find themselves forced into uncongenial environments, fighting against the odds. This problem of the tragic tension between the individual and their unfavourable environment acquires the dimensions of existential angst.

WORKS CITED

Choudhary, Bidulata. *Women and Society in the Novels of Anita Desai*. New Delhi: Creative Books, 1995.

Clement, A. "The Centre cannot Hold: The Vulnerable World of Anita Desai." *Indian Women Novelists* Set ID, Vol I. Ed. R.K. Dhawan. New Delhi: Prestige Books, 1995.

Desai, Anita. *Fire on the Mountain*. London: Penguin Book 1977. [All quotations have been derived from this edition]

Deshpande, Shashi. *The Binding Vine*. New Delhi: Penguin, 1992.

Greene, M. *Introduction to Existentialism*, Chicago: University of Chicago Press, 1950.

Gupta, Balarama G.S. "Fire on the Mountain: A Fictional Metaphor of Existentialist Philosophy." *Perspectives on Anita Desai*. Ed. Ramesh K. Srivastava, Ghaziabad: Vimal Prakashan, 1984.

Indira, S. *Anita Desai as an Artist*. New Delhi: Creative Book, 1994.

Jena Seema. *Voice and Vision of Anita Desai*. New Delhi: Ashish Publishing House, 1989.

Krishnaswamy, Shantha. *The Woman in Indian Fiction in English*. New Delhi: Ashish Publishing House, 1983.

Macquarrie, John. *Existentialism*. Harmondsworth: Penguin Books, 1972.

Misra, Parvati. *Class Consciousness in the Novels of Kamala Markandaya*, New Delhi: Atlantic Publishers and Distributors, 2001.

Nair, N. Ramachandran. "*In Custody*: The Road Not Taken." *Indian Women Novelists,* Set 1, Vol. IV. Ed. R.K. Dhawan. New Delhi: Prestige Book, 1991.

Patil, P.F. "The Wheel Turn: Central Theme in *The Village by the Sea*." *Indian Women Novelists,* Set I, Vol. IV. Ed. R.K. Dhawan. New Delhi: Prestige Book, 1991.

Prasad, Madhusudan. *Anita Desai: The Novelist*, Allahabad: New Horizon, 1984.

Raizada, Harish "The Haunted Protagonists of Anita Desai" *Perspectives of Anita Desai*. Ed. Ramesh Kumar Srivastava, Ghaziabad: Vimal Prakashan, 1984.

Sharma, R.S. *Anita Desai.* New Delhi: Arnold-Heinemann, 1981.

Shastri, N.R. "The Narrative Strategy of Anita Desai's *In Custody*." *Osmania Journal of English Studies,* 25, 1989.

Sinha, Sunita. *Graham Greene: A Study of his Major Novels*. New Delhi: Atlantic Publishers & Distributors (P) Ltd., 2007.

Solanki, Mrinalini. "Trapped Birds." *Anita Desai's Fiction: Patterns of Survival Strategies.* New Delhi: Kanishka Publishing House, 1992.

Fictionalizing 'Faith and Failure' in the 'Select Novels' of Graham Greene

AMIT KUMAR

> I've suddenly realized that I do believe the Catholic faith. Rationally I've believed for some time, but only this evening imaginatively.
>
> —Graham Greene, letter to Vivien (undated, 1925)
>
> One can believe in every point of the Catholic faith, and yet at times like this hate the initiator of it all, of life I mean.
>
> —Graham Greene, letter to Vivien (Dec. 1925)
>
> Most people are only a very little alive; and to awaken the spiritual is a very great responsibility; it is only when they are so awakened that they are capable of real Good, but that at the same time they become first capable of Evil.
>
> —T.S. Eliot, After Strange Gods (1930)

GRAHAM GREENE is perhaps the most perplexing of all the literary converts whose works animated the Catholic literary revival in the 20th century. His visions of angst and guilt, informed and sometimes deformed by a deeply felt religious sensibility, make his novels, and the characters that adorn them, both fascinating and unforgettable. Greene's novels are concerned with presenting the deterioration in the moral sense of man. He dwells on the spiritual seediness of the twentieth century and studies and is fascinated by the idea of salvation and damnation of the sinner. Interestingly, Greene has been the source of much contention among critics. He has been lauded as a master novelist who examined the place of religion and morality in twentieth-century society; he has also been decried as a melodramatist who relied too heavily on coincidence and metaphor. His focus on religion did not deter readers or jade Greene's writings, but on the contrary, in novels such as *Brighton Rock, The Heart of the Matter, The End of the Affair, Monsignor Quixote*, and his famous work, *The Power and the Glory*, it only made them more poignant. His intense focus on moral issues, politics, and religion, mixed with suspense and adventure, became the trademark of Graham Greene's ingenious works. Greene is regarded as a 'Catholic writer.' However, Greene objected strongly to being described as a Roman Catholic novelist rather he saw himself as a novelist who happened to be Catholic. A writer of religious doubt rather than certainty, Greene was less interested in the rituals and practice of Catholicism than in the moral questions it raised.

As mentioned above, we see that despite being acknowledged as a Catholic writer, Greene sees himself as a writer who happens to be a Catholic. There exists a remarkable difference between the two phrases. Many Catholics maintain that "the function of the Catholic writer [is] to produce only advertising brochures setting out the attractive terms the advantages of Church membership" (Waugh, 1948, 361). According to Waugh's definition of a Catholic, the job of the Catholic writer is to show the world why everyone should be Catholic. Greene wrote his novels, not as a Catholic but as a writer, to convey through his story aspects of the Catholic life such as Church, God and Sin. However, the stories do not always follow the doctrine of the church, and they do not always show the positive aspects of Catholic life. Greene's novels show people at their basest and in their most reviled states but they are all tempered with a Catholic conscience; a conscience that sets the characters on a path of internal struggle and ultimately understanding and faith. The Catholic conscience begins with a belief in God and builds upon the teachings of Christ. Greene's belief in God is the beginning of his Catholic conscience. Graham Greene's Catholic conscience can be seen working in the characters; though they question God, they doubt, and they suffer, the protagonists know what is right. And when they transgress they know it because through it all God is the backdrop that holds the novels together. The novels as they are would not exist without the presence of God interlaced through them; a latticework that cannot be seen but, unseen, holds the entirety together.

In her thought-provoking study, *Graham Greene: On the Frontier: Politics and Religion in the Novels*, Maria Couto claims that Greene is perhaps "the only English writer to have recognized a larger human reality." In this context, she refers to his use of Catholic themes to explore and deepen experienced reality, his sympathy for the underdog and "human inadequacy" (Couto, 1988, 259). Paul O' Prey, in his book, *A Reader's Guide to Graham Greene*, has seen Greene's Catholic novels "explore situations which reveal the conflict between the rigidity of the Church's rules..." (Prey, 1988, 82). Greene is always questioning "text-book moral theology which...has turned religion 'into a kind of police system" (Prey, 1988, 83). Greene questions the basic principles of Catholicism while maintaining his faith. He demonstrates that one need not be confined to theological rigidity; one can question the mandates of the church and still retain a belief in God. Greene distrusted theologians in general and this can be seen also in the characters Greene creates. The questions Greene raises in his novels have been seen by some to point to Greene's "surrendering to skepticism and abandoning his faith," but Joseph Pearce, in his book *Literary Converts*, believes, "if anything he surrendered to faith without abandoning his skepticism." Pearce believes Greene never lost his faith, though it may have waned at times in his life. When Graham Greene died, he still professed himself Catholic; this in itself should be proof of his Catholic status. "Greene," remarks, Pearce, "spent most of the century as a Catholic, having embraced the faith as a young man in 1926, but was continually and restlessly searching for aspects of the truth outside the church" (Pearce, 2006, 410).

Graham Greene has been seriously examined as the most significant Catholic novelist in England comparable to Francois Mauriac in France. In the early 1930s, Greene was seen mainly as a writer of thrillers and entertainments such as *Stamboul Train* (1932) and *A Gun for Sale* (1936). This perception changed with the publication of *Brighton Rock* (1938), which, while retaining the structure and atmosphere of the thriller, dealt explicitly with serious issues of Catholic morality. Greene's exploration of Catholic themes continues and intensifies in *The Power and the Glory* (1940), *The Heart of the Matter* (1948), and *The End of the Affair* (1951), quickly leading to a notion of Greene as a so-called Catholic novelist.

Catholicism is perhaps one of the most controversial aspects of Graham Greene's work. Critics like Anthony Burgess, Frederick Karl and many others who have a keen interest in the depiction of Catholic ideas in literature emphasize that since Greene is himself a catholic convert, he is at his best in those novels that deal with the principles and prejudices of the Catholic faith. However, critics like David Lodge and John Atkins adopt the view that if Greene may be called a "Catholic" writer it is because his greatest works revolve around characters and situations deeply concerned with the teachings of Catholicism. He is first and foremost a creative artist, and he appeals to all types of readers, whether they are Catholics or not.

Thus, Graham Greene remains an astounding Catholic, one who truly understood the capacity of God's love. He thought outside the conventional boundaries of Catholicism and extended the frontiers of Catholic imagination. Greene was able to conceive of "the appalling strangeness of the mercy of God" (Greene, 1938, 246). Through these words spoken by the priest in *Brighton Rock*, Greene indicates the capacity of Christ to forgive and our tendency of underestimating both God's capacity and his desire to do so. The priest could not fathom God's release of any soul. Certainly, Greene looked beyond this commonly held concept of eternal damnation and his Catholic novels reflect this. Greene referred to himself as "a Christian humanist" (Bosco, 2005, 157). For him, it seems that sin itself is not in the wrongful act but in our refusal to acknowledge the fallacies of human nature and our inability to recognize God's infinite mercy. Mark Bosco writes that the presence of God is found in the "fallen nature" of Greene's characters (Bosco, 2005, 158). Sin is not the central element of these novels, but merely serves as a catalyst. It provides a backdrop to showcase the depths of human depravity. Ultimately, the sin doesn't matter as much as recognizing one's own worth and through this recognition God's love can enter. Where God's love is, anything is possible: reform, reconciliation, redemption. Greene awakens his characters through their own suffering, brought about by the raw elements of the human condition. Greene's use of catholic themes such as sin, self-sacrifice, death by suicide, damnation and extramarital sex as a grave sin direct us towards the religious dimensions and shades of catholic imagination in Graham Greene's so-called "Catholic" novels like *Brighton Rock, The Power and the Glory, The Heart of the Matter* and *The End of the Affair.*

Through the characterization of the evil Pinkie in *Brighton Rock*, Greene visits the issues of sacrifice and suicide. This self-centred young hit man is newly married to Rose. She feels committed to him in life and in death, mostly because they feel that the consummation of their marriage is sinful as they were not married in a church. Pinkie, due to his own unlawful activities and impending arraignment (or murder), proposes a suicide pact which Rose agrees to. Both Catholic, and thus encumbered with the "special knowledge" (Greene, 1948, 35) of their religion, she feels that her sacrifice will enable his soul to have company in the damned state to which they will both be subjected. There is a place for mercy in her sacrifice. Her innocence, her youth and her lack of love and support incite a calling for God's mercy and forgiveness.

It seems that Greene establishes a connection between sin and purpose, and uses any inherent opportunity for deeper meaning. Goodness, says Greene, "has only once found a perfect incarnation in the human body and never will again, but evil can always find a home there" (Bosco, 2005, 16). The responsibility for redemption lies with the sinner, and it is the human factor of Greene's characters, the invitation for grace to enter the cavity that sin has left in its wake, which is brought into the reader's consciousness as they contemplate the interaction of evil and wrongdoing with God's generous mercy. Greene uses suicide because it leaves no room for interpretation; it is, by all Catholic accounts, the sin that damns the soul. Pinkie knew hell, and while he accepted damnation, Greene determines that it is his drive to mistrust the concept of heaven, offered through Rose's unconditional love, that would condemn him. Yet the reader's hope for Pinkie is not damned; the priest conveys the promise of salvation when he tells Rose she "can't convey my child, nor can I or anyone else the...appalling strangeness of the mercy of God" (Greene, 2004, 266). This mercy beholds Pinkie's redemption; saved from killing himself, he is blinded by acid and runs in agony over the cliff to his death. Rose lives to visit a priest who tells her that "the Church does not demand that we believe any soul is cut off from mercy" (Greene, 2004, 266). This frees her to "hope and pray" for Pinkie's soul. Her sanctity was his gift in his pathetic life, which although unacknowledged, it will remain his gift in death.

The "whiskey priest" in The *Power and the Glory* portrays this insight too. The story, set in a part of Mexico where Catholicism was being purged, introduces the protagonist, "the whiskey priest" who has led a privileged, selfish existence as parish priest. His vices have often won in situations of temptation. Now in danger and on the run he is forced to acknowledge his values and examine his commitment to both his vocation and his beliefs. He feels shame for his drinking and fornicating, which begets a child. As his privileged position changes to one of dependency, despair and fear, he laments his earlier life and blames his current situation on his sins. Yet, meditating upon the situation, he recognizes his weaknesses as parish priest. He sees that given those easy conditions he could have done a much better job. He feels that doing nothing to excel in his role as a priest was as sinful as his current debauchery. Now, fearing for his life, his cowardice is not the sin any more than his bravery could be his redemption. His sin lies in his lack of faith and inability to put his trust in God. Interestingly, it is the recognition of this that will result in his redemption. He puts himself in mortal danger to hear the confession of the dying murderer, finally employing the aspect of his work that requires sacrifice. In this ministry, he finds satisfaction by virtue of its effort and faith. He could have refused to go but he is instilled with the necessity of being present for this sinner's confession, despite the danger to himself. Similarly, he risks his life for the sake of having wine for communion. His redemption is entwined with his sacrifice. While in prison the night before his execution, he is frightened. He thinks of his child and wants her to live forever, even at the peril of his own damnation. His absolute love for her, he realizes, is what he should feel for everyone in the world. He tries to pray for his enemies, recognizing the need for prayer. He finds he can only pray for his daughter though, something he sees as another personal failure (Greene, 1940, 208). His failure is in going empty handed to God for the only thing that mattered was to "be a saint," warranting some self-restraint and a little courage (Greene, 1940, 210). His moment of grace lies in recognizing his weaknesses and his atonement for them. It is a small thing to offer in light of the ultimate sacrifice of Christ's Passion, but it is genuine.

In *The Heart of the Matter*, it is Scobie who sacrifices himself. A clean living, law-abiding man, he is married to Louise yet has an affair while his wife is away. On hearing of her impending return he must end the affair but finds he cannot hurt either woman. It appears that Greene has portrayed Scobie as a selfless character and again, the sin of his affair is almost irrelevant given the deeper meaning of the story. It serves to consider a greater understanding of life and to contemplate God's grace; these are highlighted through Scobie's inner thoughts. At a dinner party, while the conversation is on a suicide case, Scobie laments that two thousand years of discussion sees us debating the exegesis of the Passion in the same dispassionate, disconnected manner (Greene, 1951, 193). The question around this character's suicide relates to how he died and not why, pointing the reader to re-examine the ontological question of Christ. On figuring out how Scobie can best save each woman from pain, he decides to commit suicide, making it appear as if he dies of natural causes. In this way, the affair is never found out and the women are spared the hurt and embarrassment of his indiscretions. In the setting of the novel, the drama and hysteria of the affair are shadowed by a deeper meaning. It is Greene's logic of the situation, tied in with his Catholic convictions that point to the question of sacrifice.

Scobie cannot receive communion due to his maculate soul, a source of great despair for him. The exile he feels from the communion of God is more painful than death. Herein lies his damnation. No longer feeling a sense of belonging, his hell is caused by the inability to partake in communion which is his gift from God. Whatever sin he committed is irrelevant and petty compared to this damnation of loss. When he is forced to either take communion or have his indiscretions revealed to his wife, he offers up his eternal life, sacrificing it rather than to cause her pain. The sacrifice is more pertinent than the sin, which serves as an entry point for something more meaningful. Scobie takes on the role that Jesus did, at one point seeing himself as the cross (Greene, 1951, 225). It is in the element of choice that we are compelled to reflect upon the gift of salvation and its implications. Again, Greene calls for the contemplation of God's "appalling strangeness for mercy." Even in suicide, 'the unforgivable sin' (Greene, 1951, 190), Scobie channels the question of mercy. God sometimes broke his own rules, says Scobie, and would find it possible to "put a hand of forgiveness into the suicidal darkness" (Greene, 1951, 190). Christ, Scobie points out, was not murdered, as God cannot be murdered, and so Christ hung himself on the cross (Greene, 1951, 190). Despite his free will, he did that for us. Greene compels us to reflect on this. In Scobie's damnation the reader is reminded of the mistake of confusing happiness and love. One does not guarantee the other, as the crucifixion demonstrates. Ultimately then, in Scobie's suicide, it is questionable, in light of his ethereal dialogue throughout the book, whether God could or would damn him.

Self-sacrifice is echoed in *The End of the Affair*. Sarah, the heroine, makes a pact with God that she will end her affair with her lover Maurice if his life will be spared after a bomb blast. To her amazement he is indeed alive and so she is impelled to keep her promise. She now has no choice but to believe in God, a concept that she has actively denied. For Greene, the sin of adultery is secondary, superficial even. His imagination takes him beyond the pedantic results of these earthly acts; he is interested in the esoteric nature of the pain and suffering that results from them. Again, the sins are just catalysts for meaning. He uses Sarah's unexpected knowledge of God to open up the idea of sacrifice. She understands that her attempts at love were pathetic up to this point but that her capacity to love is huge. However, for it to be in any way significant, it must involve pain. As she talks to God she says:

> Dear God, I've tried to love and I've made such a hash of it. If I could love you, I'd know how to love them. I believe the legend. I believe you were born. I believe you died for us. I believe you are God. Teach me to love. I don't mind my pain. It's their pain I can't stand. Let my pain go on and on but stop theirs. Dear God, if only you could come down from your Cross for a while and let me get up there instead. If I could suffer like you, I could heal like you. (Greene, 1951, 96)

And so Sarah internalizes the infinite capacity of God's love and the beauty and truth of His sacrifice. She desires it too. She verbalizes for the reader the emotion of God's love for us, and His desire to absolve our pain and isolation with his sacrificial love.

Certainly, Greene objected to being classified as a Catholic novelist, saying that "Many times since Brighton Rock I have been forced to declare myself not a Catholic writer but a writer who happens to be a Catholic" (Couto, 1988, 32). Yet Greene's objection to this label does not diminish the centrality of Catholicism to a reading of his fiction. According to Cardinal Newman, literature "is the Life and Remains of natural man, innocent or guilty" (Newman, 1976, 194), and this surely is what Greene's fiction represents throughout, as manifested in such diverse characters as Raven, Pinkie, the 'whisky priest,' Scobie, Querry, and a great many more. It is possible that what truly characterises Greene's fiction is neither Catholicism nor humanism as such, but a form of Catholic realism—or Catholic engagement with the human factor—that is as serious about the moral and religious dimension of life as it is about the social and political one. Greene's fiction, then, is Catholic in the sense that it is informed by Catholic concepts and symbols, thus turning Catholicism into what Lodge calls "a positive artistic asset" (Lodge, 1966, 6).

Thus, we see that Greene's novels, secular and religious alike, extend and clarify our understanding of the world of his imagination and furnish a coherent view of human nature in all its contradictions. Greene has himself suggested an epigraph for all the novels he has written. The lines are from *Bishop Blougram's Apology*:

> Our interest's on the dangerous edge of things.
> The honest thief, the tender murderer,
> The superstitious atheist, demi-rep
> That loves and saves her soul in new French books—

We watch while these in equilibrium keep
The giddy line midway.

REFERENCES

Bosco, Mark, *Graham Greene's Catholic Imagination*, New York: Oxford University Press, 2005.

Couto, Maria, *Graham Greene: On the Frontier*. Basingstoke: Macmillan, 1988.

———, *Graham Greene: On the Frontier: Politics and Religion in the Novels*. New York: St Martin's, 1988.

Greene, Graham, *The Power and the Glory*, Middlesex: Heinemann, 1940.

———, *Brighton Rock*, London: Heinemann, 1938/2004.

———, The Heart of the Matter, New York: Viking Press, 1948.

———, *The End of the Affair*, London: Vintage, 1951.

Lodge, David. *Graham Greene*. New York: Columbia University Press, 1966.

Newman, John Henry. *The Idea of a University*. Ed. I.T. Ker. Oxford: Clarendon, 1976.

Pearce, Joseph, *Literary Converts*, Ignatius Press, 2006.

Prey, Paul O', *A Reader's Guide to Graham Greene*, Thames & Hudson Ltd, 1988.

Waugh, Evelyn, "Felix Culpa" in *Essays, Articles and Reviews*. (This review originally appeared in *Commonweal*, in July, 1948.)

Negotiating Self-Actualization in Shashi Deshpande's *The Dark Holds No Terror* and *Roots and Shadows*

SHIVANI MALLICK

"AFTER the Booker and the Pulitzer, Indian writers have been under pressure to conform. Once our writers get over that and write honestly—doesn't matter whether a western publisher wants it or not—we'll have much better writing" (De, 2003,1). Shashi Deshpande remains indifferent to the tenets of the Western agenda and aims for an indigenous audience. As Arnab Chakladar aptly comments: ..."the very local concerns of a writer such as Deshpande, her very lack of a global address in her style or themes, unsettle the configurations of 'India' and 'Indian Literature' that are willy-nilly created by the seemingly unconscious act of text-selection.... Her writings not only expand our understanding of Indian women's literature, or of representations of women's agency, but also expand our understanding of the complex relationships that mediate community and tradition, culture and nation, and of Indian literature as a whole" (Chakladar, 2006, 94). An evolving feminist tradition in her novels cannot be ignored. For Deshpande, "writing itself is a means to self-discovery—a medium by way of which she announces ten called by the derogatory term, adige mane sahitya" (De, 2003, 1). Shashi Deshpande's aim has also been to depict and analyze the Indian woman, her conflicts against the background of coeval Indian. She has made use of her life experiences, and her works continue to make significant contribution to Indian writing in English. The issues and themes in her novels arise from the situation of woman at the cross roads of a transitional society, changing from traditional to modern. This paper explores the complexity of contemporary existence where woman is precariously poised between two worlds, one which she cannot totally reject and the other which she cannot easily accept. This is a vital phase in the evolution of a feminist consciousness in the protagonist. An increasing awareness that patriarchal forces are defacing her identity is now combined with a growing refusal to surrender to such forces. Revealing a remarkable insight into the nature of a woman's mind, she depicts woman in myriad roles—wife, mother, daughter and an individual in her own right. She always concerns herself with a woman's search for her identity. The woman in the novels of Shashi Deshpande, in order to achieve her freedom seeks marriage as an alternative to the bondage created by the parental family. The simple need to be independent eventually becomes a demand of the inflated ego and takes shape as the love for power over others. She resents the role of a daughter and looks forward to the role of a wife with the hope that her new role will help her in winning her freedom. As Prasanna Sree Sathupati observes: "The parental home symbol of tradition and old world values has no room for Shashi Deshpande's women, for they breathe the air of rituals that obstruct the growth of a woman as a being" (Sathupati, 1995, 17).

Indu and Saru seek freedom through marriage, a room of their own and autonomy. Saru's situation is explicitly described in the novel: "I had come away from my parents in a fever of excitement after the last battle. The die was cast, the decisions taken, my boats burnt. There could be no turning back. Then, this ridiculous anticlimax" (*DHNT*, 1990, 37). Saru in *The Dark Holds No Terror*, hails from a tradition bound family which leaves scars on her psyche. Sharing the similar backdrop as that of Indu, Saru has no love lost for her family, especially her mother. Treated as a second rate citizen in her own home, owing to gender discrimination, she develops a deep and severe hatred towards her mother. The sibling rivalry between herself and her brother Dhruv verges almost on the unnatural. "He is different. He's a boy," these words establish the tradition-bound Indian mother against whom Saru has to rebel all through her life. Saru goes against her family and joins medical profession. It is once again against the wishes of her mother that she marries Manohar, a man of her choice. The departure of the protagonist from the mother is the first step towards autonomy.

Defiance seems to be the second nature to Saru. She defies her mother to become a doctor, defies her caste to marry outside, and defies social conventions by using Boozie to advance her career. To her chagrin, Saru realizes that her marriage to Manu, instead of promised freedom, led her once again into unwanted bondage. Saru's success as a doctor leads to the discord in her marriage and disintegration in her relationship with Manu. Saru's success breeds insecurity in Manu and Saru recognizes the fact: Now I know that it was there it began...this terrible thing that has destroyed our marriage" (*DHNT*, 37). Intolerable as he is of Saru's importance in the role of a doctor, yet he cannot ask her to give it up. The material comforts he hesitates to do without. Instead he tries to soothe his male ego by physically asserting himself over her. His transformation from a doting husband into a sadist invokes terror in the heart of Saru and she comes to detest the very word love: "Love…how I scorned the word" (*DHNT*, 65). Despite her hatred of Manu's physical sadism Saru refuses to take any action and loathes to admit failure. Saru refrains herself from announcing it to the world that her marriage has been a failure. She admits: "I have been clinging to the tenuous shadow of a marriage whose substance has long since disintegrated, because I have been afraid of proving my mother right" (*DHNT*, 179). It is in order to get away from the mother who accused her of having murdered her brother that Saru marries defiantly. But even this supposition turns out to be nothing but a mirage. Undecided about her stance as a woman, Saru returns to her family house. Even the parental home does not provided the required refuge. Instead of feeling overjoyed of being home, she feels enclosed. She even fails to relate to her father: "As she drinks her tea…too sweet and strong…. He (father) sat gingerly on the edge of his chair like an unwilling host entertaining an unwelcome guest. And that I suppose is what I really am. What gave me the idea that I could come back? (*DHNT*, 14). Saru's feeling of homelessness is an affirmation of her sense of seclusion. Saru leaves home twice in the novel to seek release, once to establish her independence from mother's suppression and the second time to establish her indispensability to her husband and children. The home-hunt is in essence a peace-hunt. Home is what one makes of any house. Saru could once make a happy home of just a room with Manu. It was a time when the external world did not matter at all to them and it is not healthy to live in seclusion. How they can relate to the external world and yet be an organic unit is what home is all about. One has to be at peace with oneself, to be at peace with others. Despite her driving need for a stretching hand, a comforting touch, Saru refuses to be let down by the feeling of aloneness. She takes stock of herself: "All right, so I'm alone. But so's every one else. Human beings… they're going to fail you. But because there's just us, because there's no one else, we have to go on trying. If we can't believe in ourselves, we're sunk" (*DHNT*, 200). The perfect partnership between Madhav and the father is a demonstration of the meaningful interdependence. It is a perfect pattern where they make no demand to each other.

Suddenly, it comes to her that neither Manu nor her father can be her refuge. She has to seek her own refuge and find her true self. This journey into herself, this self-exploration (search for identity) reveals her that she has to be at peace with herself before achieving anything. She decides not to pretend and struggle anymore as it only brings solace and loneliness. Integrity is the key to wholeness and this she realizes: "The guilty sister, the undutiful wife…all persons spiked with guilt. Yes, she was all of them, she would not deny that now. She had to accept these selves to become whole again. But if she was all of them, they were not all of her. She was all that and so much more" (*DHNT*, 207). Learning truth by oneself is the first step towards autonomy and Saru is able to achieve this. Her earlier doubts as to retaining her professional integrity as a doctor evaporate in thin air as she tends, confidently, to Sunita's illness. She tells her father: "And oh yes, Baba, if Manu comes, tell him to wait. I'll be back as soon as I can" (*DHNT*, 202). With this self-realization occurs the tacit understanding that any meaningful relationship is interdependent. Integration alone would make her whole again and confrontation of the disintegrating elements alone would make that possible. Escapism is no permanent solution nor should one look to anything outside of oneself to provide the solution but seek it within.

The title of the novel effectively presents the need for confrontation in terms of light and darkness. Saru's caution to Dhruv: "the dark holds no terrors. That the terrors are inside us all the time. We carry them with in us, and like traitors, they spring out when we least expect them, to scratch and maul" (*DHNT*, 76-77) is what she needs to apply to herself. In a world slowly opening out doors of opportunity to women, the urge to extend themselves beyond the confines of domesticity is very real for many educated women. Saru in *The Dark Holds No Terrors*, and Indu in *Roots and Shadows* are on the surface, successful emancipated women with fulfilling careers; Shashi Deshpande shows that in reality, they have not yet emotionally extricated themselves from patriarchal impositions, both direct and indirect.

Shashi Deshpande's heroines reject rituals that are vestiges of the past. Indu in *Roots and Shadows* wanted to explore the inner struggle of her. She represents a set of the modern women who are educated and are very much in contact with the society, dealing with the critical problems like love, sex marriage, settlement and individuality. Indu reviews everything with reason. She analyzes the ideals of detachment and freedom and tries to achieve them. She tries to listen to the voice of her conscience and revolts. Indu is projected against the women belonging to the older generation. To an old generation, a woman's life is nothing but to get married, to bear children, to have sons and then grandchildren and the ideal woman is the one who does not have her own independent identity. Indu wanted to protest against these conventional laws which are moulding the female character as only symbols of lust. In *Roots and Shadows*, Indu too searches for release from the constraints of the tradition-bound institution of marriage in search of an autonomous self. The realization of the need to conform for survival and the awareness that conformity is the great destroyer of selfhood, and the only self that can be achieved is the self-born in interpersonal relationship make Indu cry: "This is my real sorrow that I can never be complete in myself, there was somewhere outside me a part of me without which I remained complete, then I met Jayant, and lost the ability to be alone" (Deshpande, 1992, 34).

Highly sensitive, intelligent and educated, Indu could be said to be a representative of modern young woman. Indu, a middle-class young girl, brought up in an orthodox Brahmin family, headed by Akka, the mother surrogate in the novel, left home full of hatred for the family, for Akka specially and she had sworn never to go back. Indu, who had lost her mother at birth, identifies throughout the novel, Akka as the mother figure. She revolts against Akka, her world, her values and marries Jayant against the wishes of Akka. In marrying Jayant, Indu had thought that she had found her alter ego—had found in him a spiritual and psychological level of closeness. But marriage with Jayant had forced her to realize that self is an elusive centre that one could never exchange roots with another that this was an illusion and she felt cheated. Losing her own identity and living in the wake of her husband troubles her enormously. She does not find herself modern young woman any different from her mother. There is no doubt that she loves Jayant and wants him by her side at all times. But the self-same love seems to be shackling her to his side and is preventing her from taking stock of her as a separate entity: "What I feel for Jayant.... Can I compress all of it within this world. It is much more, so overwhelming a response of the whole of me to him. Sometimes I wonder if I will love him one day and live by myself. The only way in which I can be myself, my whole self again" (*RS*, 1992, 97).

Unable to come to terms with either her love for Jayant or her true self, Indu finds herself stifled and suppressed. Her marriage, she finds, is robbing her of her identity as a person apart and separating from her husband. Feeling entrapped yet she hesitates to come out of her entanglements. Her realization that she too is being moulded into the very image of woman she tried to break away from, worries her. In the first place she has broken from her family because she wanted to prove herself to be as different and as unlike as possible from women like Akka. It is her sole reason for her rebelling against the family norms and marrying Jayant. But marriage to Jayant does not prove to be the heaven she hopes for and dreams of. Her return to her parental home comes as a revelation to Indu. The feeling of homelessness is indicative of inner disintegration. Tension between the different parts with in one's self takes away the harmony with in and without. The novel gains its feminist stance in Indu's exploration into her self but it also moves beyond the boundaries of feminism into a perception of the very predicament of the human existence. Shashi Deshpande suggests that Indu has learnt to see not only her life full of possibilities for growth and grace, but the very meeting of life itself. At the end of the novel, Indu realizes that Akka is not as sadist as thought earlier, Indu has confronted her real self and she knows her roots.

The women in *Roots and Shadows*, and *The Dark Holds No Terrors*, do not present themselves as the women who want to go in self-quest, and are free from the restrictions imposed by society, culture, nature and are also free from their own fear and guilt. *Roots and Shadows* deals with a woman's attempt to assert her individuality and realize her freedom. It depicts how it brings her into confrontation with family, with male-dominated society. Indu's struggle for selfhood, her struggle towards liberation of the mind, her struggle for an emotional and intellectual definition of herself as a self-actualizing person, is in a sense to fight against her womanhood. Indu refuses to be the mother of a child that is not wholly welcome in a marriage that has become non-real because love is non-real in a marriage and that, therefore, makes her feel trapped in a negative situation since it threatens her positive struggle for independence, for selfhood, and her effort at intellectual liberation.

Indu's dilemma expresses Shashi Deshpande's feminist policies against gender roles imposed upon women in a patriarchal culture. Ever ready to please Jayant, Indu acquiesces to his desires. Indu gradually realizes that she does not exist for her but for Jayant, the archetypal male, imperialistic and subjugating. She feels in her a sense of existential insecurity, but she ultimately realizes that she has been chasing shadows, leaving her roots far behind in the family and in Jayant too. Naren, with whom she develops an adulterous relationship, is nothing more than a mere shadow to her. He has no permanent place in her memory. She realizes that marriage had stunted and hampered her individuality because she had regarded it as a trap and not as a bond. She realizes that each time, she had cut off some part of her real self to please Jayant, but this had turned their marriage into a farce. Thus, Indu's uncompromising and paradoxical feminine self that frantically longed for self-expression, finally finds its roots in the home and with her husband. Shadows disappear from her vision and she sees the clear light of day with the realization and discovery of her identity. The meek, docile and humble Indu of the early days finally emerges as a bold, challenging, conscious and rebellious woman. She resigns her job, thus defying the male authority, hierarchy and the irony of a woman's masked existence. Her self-discovery is the frightening visions of the feminine self's struggle for harmony and sanity. She comes out of her emotional upheaval, and decides to lead a meaningful life with her husband. The home she had discarded becomes the place of refuge, of solace and consolation. It is Akka's house which offers her ample opportunities to know herself. It is here that she is able to discover her roots as an independent woman, as a daughter, as a mother and as a commercial writer. The end of the novel sees a new Indu-determined, free and always in search to make her marriage work, but on new terms. She decides to spend the money; Akka has left her the way she wants and not according to other people's wishes. She finds personal freedom and completeness. Indu now takes matters into her own hands; she faces the fact of her own fault in her problems with Jayant. She will now try to save her marriage, but without compromising her principles or her individuality. Through the character of Indu, Shashi Deshpande has represented the new woman who is aware of her situation, her quest, her identity, her place and her role in the family and in society.

Shashi Deshpande's protagonists often end up discovering good traits in people whom they had earlier dismissed as selfish or cruel. Similarly, they also discover the seamy side of those whom they had all along taken as angels of love or fair play. Shashi Deshpande does not believe in portraying her characters in black and white. After their circuitous journey through life and marriage, her protagonists, who have started their journey from their parental homes in search of the freedom of the self, come to realize. They struggle to transcend the restrictive roles. They rebel, reject and seek freedom from the traditional norms and way of life. If the bonds that bind human life help individuals in continuing their lives despite the betrayals and cruelties associated with human survival, everybody has a life of one's own to live. Thus, we see that Deshpande has tried to show how her women characters reject the established hierarchical, patriarchal system and how they vehemently deny the supposed supremacy of masculine power and authority.

NOTES AND REFERENCES

Chakladar, Arnab. "Of Houses and Canons: Reading the Novels of Shashi Deshpande." *ARIEL* 37.1 (2006): 81-97.

Chatman, Seymour. *Story and Discourse: Narrative Structure in Fiction and Film*. London: Cornell University Press, 1978.

De, Aditi. "Breaking that long silence." Hindu [Bangalore] 28 Aug 2003, online ed.: 1. Web. 1 April, 2011.

Deshpande, Shashi. *The Dark Holds No Terrors* (New Delhi: Penguin Books, 1990), hereafter cited in the chapter (*DHNT*).

———. *Roots and Shadows* (Hyderabad: Disha Books, 1992), hereafter cited in the chapter (*RS*).

Sathupati Prasanna Sree. "Conflict and Identity in Shashi Deshpande's Novels", *Indian Women Novelists*: Set III: Vol. 4, ed. by. R.K. Dhawan (New Delhi: Prestige Books, 1995).

A Deconstructive Criticism of Jayanta Mahapatra's *Hunger*

PRIYANKAR DUTTA

INTRODUCTION

MY paper is about the deconstructive criticism of Jayanta Mahapatra's poem *Hunger*. Before doing the stated work I shall define Deconstruction at first.

A Japanese friend of Jacques Derrida with whom Deconstruction is associated once asked him to suggest an approximate definition of the term 'Deconstruction'. Derrida replied, "All sentences of the type 'Deconstruction is X or Deconstruction is not X', a priori miss the point, which is to say that they are at least false. As you know one of the principal things at stake in what is called in my texts Deconstruction is precisely the delimiting of Ontology and…the third person present indicative S is P". In questioning ontology, i.e. the science dealing with the essence of things Derrida is questioning the possibility that anything can have a stable and concrete essence which can be represented or defined in a linguistic or any other system. Derrida has always resisted attempts to reduce Deconstruction to a concept definable in terms of a method or technique because it is precisely the idea or assumption that meaning can be grasped in the form of some proper self-identical concept that Derrida is most determinedly out to deconstruct. Jonathan Culler defines Deconstruction rather negatively: "Deconstruction is most simply defined as critique of the hierarchical oppositions that have structured Western thought: inside/outside, mind/body, literal/metaphorical, speech/writing, presence/absence, nature/culture, form/meaning" (p. 127). J. Hills Miller says, "Deconstruction is not a dismantling of the structure of a text, but a demonstration that has already dismantled itself" (cit. Abrams 60). Paul de Maṇ says that Deconstruction "always has for its target to reveal the existence of hidden articulations and fragmentations within assumed monadic totalities". Barbara Johnson defines Deconstruction in the following way: "Deconstruction is not synonymous with destruction, however. It is in fact much closer to the original meaning of the word 'analysis' itself which etymologically means 'to undo' (p. 5). To sum up it may be said that Deconstruction as a literary theory involves a 'close reading' of the texts in order to demonstrate that any given text has irreconcilably contradictory meanings rather than being a unified, logical whole.

THE THEORY OF DECONSTRUCTION

Now I shall discuss about the theory of Deconstruction. As a theory Deconstruction is philosophical rather than literary. The philosophical ideas of Derrida have been used in reading literary texts. Viewed historically Deconstruction has its origin in October 1966 during the Symposium on "The Language and Sciences of Men". In this symposium Derrida presented his now famous *Structure, Sign and Play in the Discourse of Human Sciences* in which he attacked the traditionalist position in general and the Levi-Strauss version of Structuralism in particular. Derrida's opposition to and critique of the structuralist project begins with the observation that all analyses imply that they are based on some secure ground, 'a centre' that is outside the system under investigation and gurantees its intelligibility. Such a secure ground for Derrida is a philosophical fiction. That is to say there is no fixed or definite structure. Derridean Deconstruction is aimed against Western philosophy. In this traditional philosophical opposition "we have not a peaceful co-existence of facing terms but a violent hierarchy". According to Derrida in Western culture people think and seem to express their thoughts in terms of binary oppositions such as speech/writing, presence/absence, conscious/unconscious, etc. These binaries are actually hierarchies. Of particular interest is the speech/writing binary because involves the language in which other dichotomies are expressed. Derrida calls the Western culture phonocentric because of its tendency to privilege speech over writing. This phonocentric character is partly responsible for its logocentric character, i.e. the belief that all creative Beginning requires spoken words announced by an ideal present God. Derrida coins the term 'supplement' as the alternative of 'phonocentricism'. 'Supplement' is derived from the French verb 'suppleer' which means to take the place of as well as to supplement. Thus, it is implied that writing both supplements and takes the place of speech. Derrida refers to Rousseau's *Confessions* to substantiate the same point. Although Rousseau condemned writing as "a corruption of...speech", he admitted that he often blurted out exactly the wrong thing in public and expressed himself better in writing. Derrida has used 'differance' as the alternative of 'logocentricism'. 'Differance' conveys the fusion of the two senses of the French verb 'differer': 'to defer' and 'to be different'. A 'sign' according to this principle is something which is not like another 'sign' and something which is not the 'sign'. Thus 'differance' sees meaning as unstable and volatile. Although Derrida has deconstructed numerous texts such as the philosophical texts of Plato, Descartes, Hegel, Husserl, Rousseau, Heidegger, Saussure, Foucault, Levi-Strauss *et al.*, he does not claim to have explained or revealed their true meaning, at least in any traditional sense. In fact Derrida would deny that any 'true meaning' can be found. The central point of Derrida's theory is that one cannot make out the meaning of a text by referring to anything outside the text. So Derrida observes: "il n'y a pas de hors texte" or alternatively "il n'y a rien hors du texte" (cit. Cuddon p. 210). The self-contradictory elements in the text include what is not in the text or what is outside the text. So Derrida says, "de hors de texte" (cit. Cuddon p. 211). Though the concept of "de hors de texte" comes into direct clash with that of "il n'y a pas de hors texte" or "il n'y a rien hors du texte", the latter should be taken as the sine-qua-non of Deconstruction. What is not said or what is outside the text constitutes a 'gap', 'lacuna' or 'aporia'. In order to clarify other aspects of Deconstruction Derrida has used two more terms—'dissemation' and 'trace'. By 'dissemation' Derrida refers to the spilling of meaning—the excess of meaning which is inherent in the use of all languages. According to Derrida every 'sign' contains the 'trace' of other signs which differ from itself. Quite paradoxically the trace is not there. Thus, Derrida's theory of Deconstruction divides criticism into two categories—metaphysical and deconstructive.

The influence of Derrida is significant on the American critics, especially Paul de Man. De Man's difference from Derrida emerges when he criticizes or seems to criticize Derrida's reading of Rousseau in *Rhetoric of Blindness*. He first says that Derrida fails to see that Rousseau escapes from the logocentric fallacy precisely to the extent that his language is 'literary' and that Derrida "remains unwilling or unable to read Rousseau as literature". It is true that de Man takes the edge off this criticism by saying that Derrida's misreading of Rousseau—his "deconstructing a pseudo-Rousseau" by means of insights that could have been gained from the 'real' Rousseau—is "too interesting not to be deliberate". But it is not clear that this suggestion about Derrida's intentions is more than a courteous gesture. Perhaps the greatest difference between the two men is that Derrida resists both the existentialist pathos of early Heidegger and the apocalyptic hopelessness of late Heidegger, whereas de Man exhibits both.

J. Hills Miller represents one extreme of the deconstructionist movement—its extreme de Manian wing. He applies deconstructive analysis to prose fiction. He is known especially for his application of this type of critical reading to prose fiction. His statement of his critical practice indicates how drastic the result may be of applying to works of literature the concepts and procedures that Derrida had developed for deconstructing the foundations of Western metaphysics. His conclusion is that any literary text as a ceaseless play of 'irreconcilable' and 'contradictory' meanings is 'indeterminate' and 'undecidable'; hence; that "all reading is necessarily misreading".

The other extreme of the deconstructionist movement is represented by Stanley Fish. His connections with the movement are loose and he is not usually thought of as a deconstructionist, nor would he describe himself to be so. But because he has become identified with the claim that no text can determine its own interpretation, the enemies of the movement have given him honorary membership in it. Such an assimilation is plausible, inasmuch as Fish wholeheartedly accepts the view of language common to Derrida, Wittgenstein and Davidson. Fish, however does not find this view startling, nor does he view it either as having important ethical consequences or as dictating critical practice. He and Miller agree that language is a play of differences, that no word is given meaning simply by the presence of a referent and that objectivity is never more than inter-subjectivity. But unlike Miller and de Man, Fish does not think of literature as an area in which a special kind of language is used, nor as an area of culture which has a permanent quarrel with another called philosophy. Unlike Heidegger and Derrida he does not see the end of the metaphysics of presence as a world-historical event; but merely as an occasion to remind literary critics that there is no point in putting the text in as many contexts as anyone finds it useful to put it in. Fish characterizes himself as a pragmatist. His view of the relation between philosophy and literary criticism has much in common with that of John Searle: both men would say that the shipwreck of the philosopher's traditional fundamentalist projects and the absence of what Fish calls 'determinate meaning' has no dramatic consequences for the work of the literary critic. For Seale and Fish, if one has Wittgenstein one does not really need Derrida, although one might still welcome his company. Yet Fish can be seen as writing in one of the veins in which Derrida himself writes, albeit a very different vein from that of either de Man or Miller. When Fish criticizes the attempt at 'determinate meaning' by saying that "whatever they do, it will only be interpretation in another guise because, like it or not, interpretation is the only game in town" he is resisting the central thesis of Derrida's *Structure, Sign and Play* the thesis that we must give up the 'the concept of centered structure' the "concept of a play based on a fundamental ground, a play based on the basis of a fundamental immobility and a reassuring certitude , which itself is beyond the reach of play". This thesis would be accepted by a large number of critics who like Fish would not care to be labeled 'deconstructionists' but who would be happy to grant that deconstructionism is playing an important and useful role in literary studies. That role is to free us from the notion of the correct interpretation of the text—the one dictated by the text itself and from the idea that literary criticism needs to be put on the secure path of a science by adopting some such ideal of correctness.

THE WORKING OF DECONSTRUCTION

Now I shall discuss how Deconstruction works. Gayatri Chakraborty Spivak gives one of the best accounts as to how Deconstruction works: "If in the process of deciphering of a text in the traditional way we come across a word that seems to harbor an unresolvable contradiction, and by virtue of being one word is made sometimes to work in one way and sometimes in another and thus is made to point away from the absence of a unified meaning, we shall catch at that word. If a metaphor seems to suppress its implications, we shall catch at that metaphor. We shall follow its adventures through the text and see the text coming undone as a structure of concealment, revealing its self-transgression, its undecidability." Barbara Johnson has something interesting to say: "The Deconstruction of a text does not proceed by random doubt or arbitrary subversion but by the careful teasing out of the warring forces of signification within the text itself" (p. 5). Chris Barker is more explicit when he says, "Deconstruction involves the dismantling of hierarchical conceptual oppositions such as man/woman, black/white, reality/appearance, nature/culture, reason/madness, etc. which serve to gurantee truth by excluding and devaluing the 'inferior' part of the binary. Thus, speech is privileged over writing, reality over appearance, men over women" (p. 32). M.H. Abrams goes one step further when he says, "Typically a deconstructive reading sets out to show how that conflicting forces within the text itself serve to dissipate the seeming definiteness of its structure and meaning into an indefinite array of incompatible and undecidable possibilities" (p. 56). Barbara Johnson has enumerated seven points to guide the students to respond to what is before them on the text from a deconstructive outlook, though they cannot be said to be exhaustive in any way. They are—

(1) ambiguous words
(2) undecidable syntax
(3) incompatibilities between what a text says and what it does
(4) incompatibilities between the literal and between the figurative
(5) incompatibilities between explicitly foregrounded assertions and illustrative examples or less explicitly asserted supported material
(6) obscurity and
(7) fictional self-interpretation.

To sum up to deconstruct a discourse is to show how it undermines the philosophy it asserts or the hierarchical opposition on which it relies by identifying the text and then dismantling the rhetorical operations that produce the supposed ground of argument, the key concept or premise.

APPLICATION

Before making a deconstructive criticism of Jayanta Mahapatra's *Hunger,* it is customary to present the argument of the poem under review. Broadly speaking the argument of the poem just mentioned runs thus:

In the first stanza the speaker confesses that one day he was consumed with fleshly desires. A fisherman whom he met by chance offered him his daughter for a few rupees. The fisherman spoke very casually to the speaker while making the bargain. He was poor and was in need of money. He had no other way but to sacrifice the youth of his daughter to serve his purpose. In the next stanza the bargain being finalized, the speaker followed the fisherman across the vast sandy shore. Though the speaker was aware of the enormity of his crime which he was going to commit, his body was torn with sexual hunger. In the third stanza the speaker, led by the fisherman, arrived at the latter's cottage. For the speaker the cottage seemed to be a wound because he was aware of the sinful act he was going to make. The sense of the wind, the days and the nights were obliterated to him. Ferns scratched his skin. Inside the shabby cottage an oil lamp burned. The soot was on the wall and the soot seemed to affect his mind. In the fourth stanza, the fisherman informed the speaker that his daughter was fifteen years old. Then he left the speaker to feel his daughter saying that he would come back soon. The speaker had a sense of catastrophe falling on him. The discovery of tricks in the words and activities of the fisherman shocked the speaker. He found the body of the girl as cold as rubber. However, sex hunger tormented him and he felt a fish moving and turning inside him. The two hungers—hunger for sex on the part of the speaker and hunger for food on the part of the fisherman—became mixed here.

Now I shall make a deconstructive criticism of the poem just mentioned. "A New Critical reading of the text", i.e. the central tension at work in the text and how it is resolved, as Lois Tyson observes, is often "a useful step in deconstructing a literary work" (p. 262). Following this principle we can say that the central tension at work in *Hunger* is between the speaker's hunger for sex and the fisherman's hunger for food. As we see the situation from the speaker's point of view, it is safe to say that the speaker's hunger for sex privileges over the fisherman's hunger for food. It is true, at least to some extent, as the fisherman nowhere speaks of his hunger for food—the compulsion for which he has to satisfy the speaker's hunger for sex through his daughter—but helps the speaker spontaneously so that the later's hunger is fully satisfied.

> "......: my daughter, she's just turned fifteen...
> Feel her. I'll be back soon, your bus leaves at nine."

Here very cleverly he suggests the youth of his daughter and shows his time sense so that he can give his customer all-round service.

A deconstructive criticism will try to show that the text reverses this hierarchy of the hunger for sex over the hunger for food. Before trying to find out such a contradictory perspective I shall analyse what the poet himself says about this poem. About the poem *Hunger* Jayanta Mahapatra says:

> The poem is based on a true incident; it could easily have happened to me on the poverty-ridden sands of Gopalpur-on-sea. Often have I imagined myself walking these sands, my solitude and my inherent sexuality working on me, to face the girl inside the dimly-lit, palm frond shack.

There is a contradiction in Mahapatra himself as "true incident" collides with "could easily have happened" and "imagined". This contradictory attitude is also found in the text itself and it is such an attitude which is the key to a deconstructive criticism. In an attempt to oppose the privileging the speaker's hunger for sex over the fisherman's hunger for food it can be said that the fisherman is hardly given a voice. He speaks very few words and that too about the speaker's 'hunger' and its materialization:

> … … will you have her… …

In spite of this verbal/literal absence, the fisherman is metaphorically present in the text by being the very consciousness about the conscience of the speaker. Though the fisherman speaks nothing of his 'purpose' of selling the youth of his daughter and in fact speaks 'carelessly' the speaker discovers some purpose behind the deal made by the fisherman even at the cost of his own uneasiness;

> … … … as though his words
> Sanctified the purpose with which he faced himself

Then though the fisherman behaves like an expert businessman throughout, never suggesting his moral scruple, the speaker discovers a mental struggle going in the fisherman:

> I saw his white bone thrash his eyes.

Actually the speaker discovers his own mental struggle between action and passivity in the fisherman. The conflict going between 'mind' and 'flesh' in the speaker has been beautifully dramatized by the verb 'thumping':

> My mind thumping at the flesh's sling.

The same internal conflict perturbs the speaker even when he thinks of burning the house as a gesture of self-repentance but not of postponing the call of his 'flesh'. The pressure of the conflict is so much that the speaker seems to lose his identity:

> The wind was I, and the days and nights before.

Then the speaker mentions of 'palm fronds', 'shack' and 'sticky shoot'. Such a mention is unnecessary in a poem dealing with one's hunger for sex and yet they are referred to by the speaker to give the readers an impression of the fisherman's poverty in general and his hunger for food in particular. The discovery of 'wile' in the words of the fisherman is shocking to him because this artificiality contrasts with his genuine sexual passion. The inevitable disappointment follows:

… … her years were cold as rubber.

Not only that the legs of the fisherman's daughter appear to him to be wormy, meaning abject like a worm.

Thus the above discourse proves that the speaker's hunger for sex is sometimes minimized by the fisherman's hunger for food. Bruce King rightly says, "…a Mahapatra poem often deconstructs itself and what it expresses" (p. 184). To sum up in *Hunger* the speaker coming to a poor fisherman's daughter to find a fulfillment of his hunger for sex finds another hunger—the hunger for food. Such a generalization can be deconstructed with the help of Neitzsche's principle of causality. Neitzsche observes, "The fragment of the outside world of which we become conscious comes after the effect has been produced on us and is projected a posteriori as its cause". Similarly the fisherman's hunger for food is said to pave way for the speaker's gratification of sexual hunger. The logical cause comes after the effect has been produced on the speaker:

… … the fish slithering turning inside.

The word 'slithering' is suggestive of sickness inside and this is the feeling of the speaker upon realizing the real cause of the fulfilment of his hunger.

Finally a deconstructive criticism will also find the ways in which the binary opposition on which a text rests can be deconstructed: that is it can be examined to find the ways in which the opposing elements in the text overlap and are not really opposed. Chris Barker rightly says, "The purpose of deconstruction is not simply to reverse the order of binaries but to show that they are implicated in each other" (p. 32). In *Hunger*, it is at the end that this overlapping occurs:

… … I felt the hunger there
The other one, the fish slithering, turning inside.

Here "the other one" refers to the hunger for food on the part of the speaker and this hunger is symbolized by 'fish'.

Apart form this deconstructive criticism from the thematic point of view, any text can be deconstructed from the technical point of view as well though in some cases the examples, not exactly the points will overlap. A deconstructive criticism in this method as Peter Barry points out "may not constitute a complete break with the more familiar forms of criticism" (p. 74). Barry calls the three stages of this deconstructive process the verbal, the textual and the linguistic ones.

The verbal stage is very similar to the conventional pattern of reading, expounded in William Empson's *Seven Types of Ambiguity* and elsewhere. It involves looking in the text for paradoxes and contradictions at what might be called the purely verbal level. For example, in Jayanta Mahapatra's *Hunger* the expression "I felt the hunger there,/ the other one,..." carries the possibility of a type of 'hunger' suggested earlier. Internal contradictions of this kind are indicative for the deconstructionist of language's endemic unreliability and slipperiness. Identifying paradoxical and contradictory expressions and phrases like this is the first step of showing that the Saussurean 'signifier' is at war with the 'signified'. Of course Derrida would opt to call such an example 'transcendental signified' by which he would mean that a 'sign' would escape the play of 'signifiers' and would have a privileged existence.

The textual stage of this method moves beyond individual phrases and takes a more overall view of the poem. At this stage the critic is looking for shifts or breaks in the continuity of the poem: these shifts reveal instabilities of attitude and hence the lack of a fixed or unified position. They may be shifts in focus, shifts in time, or tone, or point of view, or attitude, or pace, or vocabulary. They may well be indicated in the grammar, for instance in a shift from first person to third, or past tense to present. Thus, they show paradox and contradiction on a larger scale than is the case with the first stage, taking a broad view of the text as a whole. In the case of the poem under review there is an obvious shift in time. For example, the poem seems to poetize a past experience of the speaker but while some expressions uttered by the fisherman such as "Feel her" and "your bus leaves at nine" are indicative of the present, another expression attached to the expression cited just now—"I'll be back soon" is suggestive of the future time. Hence no single wider framework is provided to contextualize the speaker's hunger for sex. Again every now and then one finds a shift of focus from the speaker hunger for sex to the fisherman's hunger for food. Actually it is the consciousness of crime on the part of the speaker or rather his pricks of conscience which counts for this change of focus and sometimes the blurring of focuses so to say.

The linguistic stage finally involves looking for moments in the poem when the adequacy of language as a medium of communication is called into question. Such moments occur when, for example, there is implicit or explicit reference to the unreliability or untrustworthiness of language. It may involve, for instance, saying that something is unsayable; or saying that it is impossible to utter or describe something and then doing so; or saying that language inflates, or deflates, or misrepresents its object, and then continuing to use it anyway. If in *A Refusal to Mourn the Death, by Fire, of a Child in London* Dylan Thomas keeps on mourning inspite of almost confessing not to mourn, in the poem under review though the poet says "It was hard to believe...", what he does in this poem is that he poetizes a real incident and therefore the question of not believing what has been clearly suggested in the poem—the speaker's uncontrollable sexual urge—does not arise at all.

CONCLUSION

As the process of deconstructing the poem is over a pertinent question comes in our mind:—"What use does this strategy have for us?" In reply it can be said that Deconstruction as a process of reading a text neither explains a text nor leads us from a faulty to a correct way of thinking. Then is it not a futile exercise? To conclude the discourse and to answer the question it may be said that in the process of reversing hierarchies in the deconstructive process a whole strategy of the process of making hierarchies is uncovered and found wanting. The strategy uncovered can be roughly termed ideology and as we all know ideologies have distinct political implications. For example, in the hierarchy of the haves (the speaker having money can make a mockery of the poverty of the fisherman by making him sell the youth of his daughter for some rupees) and the have-nots (the fisherman being miserably poor has become forced to employ his daughter in earning money) was responsible for the ideology of exploitation during the colonial period. By showing the thought process which creates such a hierarchy as groundless, Deconstruction continues to counter the destructive potential of exploitative ideology. In reversing the hierarchy Deconstruction helps to initiate a process by which the economically oppressed classes can be elevated to positions of economic affluence and also reminds that the new hierarchy too is deconstructible.

WORKS CITED

Abrams, M.H. *A Glossary of Literary Terms* (8th edition, Thomson Wadsworth).

Barry, Peter. *Beginning Theory* (2nd edition. Manchester University Press).

Cuddon, J.A. *The Penguin Dictionary of Literary Terms* (4th edition, Penguin Books).

Culler, Jonathan. *Literary Theory: A Very Short Introduction.*

Johnson, Barbara. *The Critical Difference.*

King Bruce. *Modern Poetry in English* (Revised Edition, Oxford University Press).

Spivak, Chakraborty Gayatri. *Of Grammatology*. (trans).

Tyson, Lois. *Critical Theory Today: A User Friendly Guide* (2nd edition, Routledge).

STATEMENT ABOUT OWNERSHIP AND OTHER PARTICULARS OF

The Atlantic Critical Review

FORM IV

(See Rule 8)

Place of Publication	:	New Delhi
Periodicity of the Publication	:	Quarterly
Printer's Name	:	Manish Kumar
Nationality	:	Indian
Address	:	B-2, Vishal Enclave New Delhi 110027
Publisher's Name	:	Manish Kumar
Nationality	:	Indian
Address	:	B-2, Vishal Enclave New Delhi 110027
Editor's Name	:	Sunita Sinha
Nationality	:	Indian
Address	:	402, Rameshwaram Apartment, Miss Mandal Compound, East Boring Canal Road, Patna, Bihar
Names and addresses of individuals who own the newspaper and partners or shareholders holding more than one per cent of the total capital	:	K.R. Gupta B-2, Vishal Enclave New Delhi 110027

I, Manish Kumar, hereby declare that the particulars given above are true to the best of my knowledge and belief.

Sd/-

Date: 01st October, 2015

MANISH KUMAR
Publisher

A Study of Hybridity and Identity in Salman Rushdie's *The Moor's Last Sigh*

ANJU BALA AGRAWAL

SALMAN RUSHDIE, one of the most important English language novelists, has mythologized all our lives and done so in the arena of multiculturalism and postmodernism. Hybridity and identity are part of postmodernism. Almost all novels of Rushdie, from *Midnights Children* to *The Moor's Last Sigh,* hybridity is intertwined with plot. Hybridity is the negation of purity and the celebration of multiplicity and eclecticism. Akbar S. Ahmed argues that "the mixing of images, interlocking of cultures, juxtaposition of different peoples, availability of information, are partly explained because populations are mobile as never before." Hybridity is manifested in three dimension: (1) the metaphor of the palimpsest visualizes the nature of hybridity and dominates the book's cultural vision, (2) hybrid characters, (3) cultural legacies let by the British Empire are inevitably intertwined with local cultures, which illustrates that cultural hybridity is the predictable product of cultural formation.

The Moor's Last Sigh is an incestuous saga. It is after Nabokov's *Ada* and Garcia Marquez's *One Hundred Years of Solitude* which set the standard for the magic realism. There is a family chart at the beginning of this novel marking the birth and death dates and relations of the members of the Da Gama and Zogoiby families. This is useful as the book is full of intrusive outsiders as well as members of four generations of the family. Some of them stay around to become a part of the already overcrowded family and some leave the stage as abruptly as they appear. The narrator of this richly textured, densely allusive tale is Moraes Zogoiby, but the true protagonist is his mother, Aurora Da Gama. She is a crazy woman. She is a famous painter and a beautiful society woman. A giant public personality and a heroine of the nationalist movement, she is a legendary lady. She is the great creative mother figure of this novel, which, perhaps to give us a total image of itself, consistently alludes to an image of Mother India who with her garishness and inexhaustible motion loved and betrayed and ate and destroyed and again loved her children and with whom the children's passionate conjoining an eternal quarrel stretched long beyond the grave. This image, which Rushdie makes sure that even the least attentive reader will be aware of, might equally apply to Aurora. She is the daughter of a Catholic who is a pepper merchant and claims to be descended from no less a figure than Vasco da Gama. In the beginning of the novel we find a table of Family. The table starts with Francisco da Gama, grandfather of Aurora, a wealthy merchant. He was incapable of living a settled life. Aurora's grandmother, Epifania Menezes is a down to earth lady. She is faithful to "England. God Philistinism, the old ways," (18) survives to trouble succeeding generations and to utter the curse that will blight the life of unborn Moraes. Their son Camoens, after flirting with Communism, becomes a Nehru man. Camoens' daughter Aurora falls in love with a humble Jewish clerk Abraham Zogoiby. He is a Cochin Jew from a family descended from Spanish Jews expelled by the Catholics after the fall of the last Andalusian sultan. She marries to Abraham Zogoiby. Abraham, abandoning the declining Jewish community of Cochin, transfers the family business to Bombay and settles in a fashionable suburb where he involves himself into more lucrative activities: supplying girls to the city's brothels, smuggling heroin, speculating in property, trafficking in arms and eventually in nuclear weapons. Abraham is little more than a comic-book villain. On the other hand, Aurora is an emotional center of the book. She is a disracted mother. She suffers intermittent remorse for not loving her children enough, but prefers finally to see them through the lens of her art. Moraes is worked into a series of her paintings of "Mooristan", a place where "worlds collide, flow in and out of one another, and washofy away.... One universe, one dimension, one country, one dream, bumpo'ing into another, or being under, or on top. Call it Palimpstine" (226). In these paintings, with increasing desperation, she tries to paint old, tolerant Moorish Spain over India, overlaying, or palimpsesting, the ugly reality of the present with "a romantic myth of the plural, hybrid nation" (227). Her paintings of high period are darker. She pours into them not only her maternal fears but also her larger and prophetic fears for the nation. Her last painting which gives the book its title, shows her son "lost in limbo like a wandering shade; a portrait of a soul in Hell".

The novel is the history of Moraes' family and its very broad circle that incorporates all the disparate elements, both domestic and imported, that inform life in that throbbing city: Christian, Muslim, Hindu, Indian

Goan, Portuguese and on and on. Love, sex, hate, greed, jealousy, ambition and many violent aspects of life can be seen in this single family. The narrator's mother Aurora, a famous artist is at the center of the story. Her paintings suggest, in their bold colours, personal and political themes and surreal images like the paintings of Frida Kahlo. All the other family members, both antecedents and her own four children, swirl around her dazzling, outrageous and possibly dangerous personality. The narrator is her only son and youngest child, Moraes, known as "the Moor" and not the least of his problems are three sisters, Ina, Minnie and Mynah. Moraes' father builds an empire in the spice trade, finally ruling it from a sky-scraper-top botanical hothouse and living always with the uneasy suspicion that his unquenchable wife enjoys a lover or three. His sisters adopt various professions as a runaway model with a "super Sashay", a nun and a feminist activist. The eponymous Moor must cope with a clublike, unformed right hand, a limb that his mother paints into portraits in wildly fantastic images, and which, after boxing lessons from a family retainer, earns him a nickname—"The Hammer". His mind matures at a normal rate, but his body develops at a double pace.

In the family, we also find a thieving *ayah* named Miss Jaya, a tutor named Dilly Hormuz who tutors the young Moor in subjects not mentioned in her contract, a painter named Vasco Miranda who earns his fame doing airport murals. In fact, this book is an extraordinary act of imagination. We have a large number of characters. Moraes falls in love with the beautiful Uma, a deranged and brilliant young Hindu artist. Uma set herself up as a rival-personally and professionally—to his mother. Moor is quite unprepared for the onslaught of the opportunistic new India, with its artists ready to scavenge in the "dead sea" of their country's heritage. Moor is rejected by his parents as a result of Uma's mad machinations and is forced, after a terrifying stint in prison, to abandon his privileged lifestyle. He is transported to the "Underworld" over which Fielding, an ambiguously malign Hades presides. This underworld is the foundation of the world of appearance Moor formerly inhabited. His father's fortune is aided by judicious dabbling in "white powder". As Moor comes to learn: "they are not inhuman, these Mainduck-style little Hitlers and it is in their humanity that we must locate our collective guilt...for if they are just monsters...then the rest of us are excused. I personally do not wish to be excuse. I made my choice and lived my life" (297). Moor's life coincides with as era of civil discord, state repression, and the growth of a Hindu fundamentalist movement hostile to modernism and minorities like the Christian-Muslim-Jewish da Gama-Zogoibys. Toward the end of the novel, the middle-aged Moor reverses his ancestors' flight by leaving Bombay for the relative tolerance of the recently democratized Spain.

Aurora is a living example of India as a pluralistic and hybrid nation. She insists on speaking only English in her own inimitable way, "All these different lingoes cuttofy us off from one another" (179) she says. Motherhood is not her favourite role and she overshadows her three female children, "they can't growfy fast enough for me. God! how long this childhood business draggoes out. Why couldn't I have...even one child, who grew up really fast" (141). The eponymous "Moor" born in 1957 after a four and a half month pregnancy mystically fulfills his mother's rash wish aging twice as fast as normal. In his speeded up growth, which makes him bigger than every one else his age—"I was a skyscraper freed of all legal restraints, a one man population explosion, a megalopolis"—the Moor can stand as an embodiment of India itself. The link is underscored by the pulls and tugs on his loyalties, the presumptive European strain in his ancestory and the transreligion union between his Christian mother and Jewish father: "I, however, was raised neither as Catholic nor as Jew. I was both, and nothing: a jewholic—anonymous, a cathjew nut, a stewpot, a mongrel cur. I was—what's the word these days?—*atomised*. Yessir: a real Bombay mix" (104). Moraes' family line is a fuse of lost causes, with Moraes its explosive issue.

The novel is affectionately delineated, with an eye for traditional narrative detail. *The Moor's Last Sigh* is a grand family chronicle of the passionate love and business affairs of four generations of a grotesque and rich Indian family. Here Rushdie's creative power as a verbal illusionist comes forward as the novel is filled with puns and verbal games, buffoonery and scenes of slapstick comedy. *The Moor's Last Sigh* is not merely a family story but it also depicts a post-colonial society. This society is expressly located in India that has gone through diverse experiences of colonial intrusions and cultural impacts. The history of India is itself a complex one because in it transcultural activities and reciprocal influences among different cultures increasingly complicate and extend the nexus of cultures. The emotions and experiences derived from in-between struggles also permeate most of Rushdie's works. The novel represents a hodge-podge of cultures, as befits cultural hybridity in post-colonial theory. Cultural hybridity is also an in-between state that gives rise to constant oscillations between different cultures. Yet, it should be remembered that the word hybridity is not merely pointing to culture but also to race and caste. In fact, it is more important to explore the impetus that brings about hybridity. In this novel, imperialism and colonization are the significant impetus that calls forth the issue in post-colonial theory, imperialism and colonization give rise to dislocation and displacement as culture is inevitably transnational. This is well illustrated by Da-Gama-Zogoiby family of complicated descent, which means that the family is descended from diverse ancestry, including moors, Portuguese, Jews and even Moguls that once ruled India. The hybrid state makes identification more puzzling because Moraes, situated in-between these different cultural and ethnic groups, is paradoxically both included and excluded by each of them. Rushdie makes up the story with a semblance of using bits and pieces from Snow White to Ganesha.

The Moor's Last Sigh is mainly focused upon the two multicultural societies, Moorish Spain and modern India. The idea of multiculturalism is most likely to explore more meaning from Rushdie's palimpsest of Modern India over Moorish Spain. In his texts, Rushdie challenges the English/European/white sense of identity. His protagonists are engaged into a long and difficult quest for identity in a foreign country. Saladin's metamorphosis into a demon with hoofs, horns and tail, Saleem's disintegrating body in *Midnights' Children*, Moraes's freaky appearance having a clublike right hand and a metabolism that dooms him to live "double quick" aging twice as fast as ordinary human beings are but few examples of how the immigrant is both a fragile and vulnerable being. His fragility is part of his hybridity of being born across.

In the novel, there is a long quest for a stolen painting, the one which gives the novel its title in a foreign country, Spain. But the characters' quest turns to be a long search for his origins. Indeed, Zogoiby discovers that his ancestors were from Jewish, Muslim and Christian background. Moraes' identity is then a condensation of levels in the same way the painting, he lastly found, is composed of multiple layers. The origin is buried deep inside so as to be exhumed dug out "there was no doubt that the canvas was a palimpsest" (416) consequently the establishment of meaning is just a matter of hybrid construction, an archeological enterprise. In *The Moor's Last Sigh*, the narrator calls himself a "Bastard, a smelly shit" (104). Moor's identity a "high-born-cross breed" (5) is seen to parallel that of a nation with a long history of immigration and imperialism.

Rushdie pursues palimpsest with considerable vigour. He uses novelistic, historiographical and autobiographical device. Thus, Granada, Boabdil's lost capital, is also Bombay, the sighed-for home of Moraes as well as of the author over whose person he is written. "Both are cities from which a regenerative cross-fertilization of cultures might have taken place, but for ethnic and religious tolerance" (Coetzee: 14). The central metaphor of *The Moor's Last Sigh* is the idea of a palimpsest. First it is applied to Aurora's particular form of art but as the novel proceeds this metaphor is extended to cover history of India as a country and identity of the self. *The Moor's Last Sigh* is a painting by aurora but it is the title of the novel also. For the world, Abraham (Moor's father) deals in talcum powder and spices but his transactions mask his trafficking in cocaine and prostitution. To quote: "The city itself, perhaps the whole country, was a palimpsest, Under world beneath Over world, black market beneath white; when the whole life was like this, when as invisible reality moved phantom wise beneath a visible fiction, subverting all its meaning, how then could Abraham's career have been any different? How could any of us have escaped that deadly layering? … How could we have lived authentic live?" (184-85).

In the background of the novel, we find Bombay. Bombay is a city where people of different cultures and religions inhabit. In fact, Bombay is a glaring example of hybridity. It plays an important part in the plot of the story. "But then if the narrator is Bombay, Bombay is India: the bastard child of a Portuguese-English wedding, and yet the most Indian of Indian cities.... Those who hated India, those who sought to ruin it, would need to ruin Bombay" (350). The city connection is irresistible. Rushdie's relationship with Bombay is crucial. The picture of Bombay which we find in the novel has two sides. One has many headed cosmopolis of diverse cultures; this is Moraes Zogoiby's "inexhaustible city of excess" with which he tells us, he is deeply and for ever in love. The other Bombay is new one of religious and nationalistic fanaticism. New Bombay is the city of senseless bombings and the egoistic cynicism of postcolonial intellectuals and the new power elite. "The heartfelt political message of *The Moor's Last Sigh* is to defend the richness and multiplicity of the first Bombay against the assaults of the second, against the imposition of Hindi language, art and gods as "authentic", Indian culture, against fundamentalist Hindu triumphalism" (Orhan Pamuk: 3).

Thus, Moraes resembles Rushdie himself. Though Rushdie is not physically similar to his protagonist, he has had to endure the freakishness of enforced isolation. He has the ability to live a normal writer's life maimed (that club hand) by the threat of assassination. Like Moraes, Rushdie is also of mixed cultural background, although his fictional character is more exotic, with Spanish, Portguese and Moorish bloodiness complicated by a Jewish and Christian religious tolerance. Rushdie denounces the religious fundamentalism that threatens Indian society and suggests cultural hybridity as its remedy, but he also derides false, capitalist multiculturalism and in acknowledging the reality that religious identity, especially in India, marks the inevitable limit to the success of a truer form of cultural hybridity.

REFERENCES

Ahmed, Akbar S. *Postmodernism and Islam,* Routledge: London and New York, 1992, p. 26.

Coetzee, J.M. "Palimpsest Regained", The New York Review of Books, Vol. XLIII, No. 5, March 21, 1996 p. 14.

Pamuk, Orhan. "Salaam Bombay", *The Times Literary Supplement*, No. 4823, September 9, 1995, p. 3.

Rushdie, Salman. *The Moor's Last Sigh*, London: Vintage Random House, 1995. All references to the text are from this edition and have been indicated by page numbers in parentheses.

The Dramatic Techniques of Girish Karnad

SUNANDA MISHRA

GIRISH KARNAD belongs to the generation of playwrights who reshaped Indian theatre as a national institution in the later 20th century. He is a celebrated playwright, actor, script writer, and film and television director as well. He has received numerous awards for his contributions to drama, theatre and the silver screen, including the Padma Awards—Padma Shri (1974) and Padma Bhushan (1992), Kalidas Samman (1998) and the Jnanapith Award (1998), India's highest distinction for lifetime contribution to literature and the arts.

Besides depicting human emotions which lend universal appeal to his plays, the techniques Karnad employs in his plays are in conformity with Indian dramatic traditions. He explores devices of his own land and those of the West as well in order to devise a desired dramatic form, characterization, organization of incidents and their dramatic representation. He experiments boldly with the folk and classical devices. Heuses the conventions and motifs of folk theatre like masks, mime, songs, dances, curtains, the commentator-narrator, the actor-manager, puppets, dolls, horseman, the story-within-a-story, facilitating a mixture of the human and the non-human to create a queer magical world, Kannada folktales, story of cobra, a play within the play, the prologue, an epilogue and monologues in all of his plays to show the absurdity of life with all its elemental passions and conflicts, and man's eternal struggle to achieve perfection. The technique of folk theatre along with modern devices like light and sound makes his styleclose to typical Kannada and Brechtian theatre. On his dramatic technique, Karnad in his interview, says:

> …to me three kinds of theatre between which I swivelled and moved and written have been symbolized in a sense by three kinds of theatre, the Company on one side, the Yakshagana with mask-like appearance, its ritual atmosphere, on the other and thirdly the kind of theatre which really is a naturalistic theatre, the western theatre

> as one came to see it, hate it, dislike it, but was impossible not to be possessed by it. (79)

Among the various devices used by Karnad to denaturalize his theatre and make it truly indigenous, the technique of Sutradhara of the Classical tradition and the Bhagavata of the *Yakshagana* tradition is conspicuous. *Sutradhara*, like the chorus in the Greek drama, plays the role of an introducer or a commentator. On the role of *Sutradhara,* Raj Rekha Shukla writes:

> Sutradhara means literally the 'string holder', translated as 'puppet master' or 'manipulator', though he was almost certainly an actor himself and played not merely an impresario's role. He predates the Bhagavata of Yakshagana with whom he bears many similarities as controller of stage action, orchestrator of the musicians, director and choreographer of the actor-dancers and fundamentally, during the performance itself a story-teller. (182)

At the beginning of *Yayati, Sutradhara* informs the audience that the play, though deals with an ancient myth, is not a mythological one—"our play has no gods". In *Tughlaq*, he uses the announcer, who carries out numerous functions, especially that of a narrator or commentator, to reform India politically and socially. The actor-manager is used in *The Fire and the Rain* who explains that the purpose of the theatre is to get away from the dreariness of reality, boredom of modern life; it is a means of entertainment. The actor-manager talks about the profession of acting to Arvasu. *Sutradhara* in *Yayati* and *Bhagavata* in *Hayavadana* become one in *Naga-Mandala* and appear as the Story. The role of the Dolls is played by the Man and the Flames. Commenting on *Yakshagana* style adopted in *Hayavadana,* Kathrynh Ansen writes: "Based on the tale of transposed heads from the *Kathaaritsagara, Hayavadana* is a symbolic drama employing several conventions of *Yakshagana*, such as the half-curtain which is carried onstage to introduce new characters, and the Bhagavata or narrator, who introduces the story and comments on the action throughout the play" (*Asian Folklore Studies* 79).

Use of Prologue and Epilogue puts Karnad very close to the modern playwrights like Bernard Shaw. A play-within-the-play begins with the Prologue in *Naga-Mandala*. It is used to set the tone and mood of the play. He uses the Story to play the role of *Bhagavata* and Story is a woman character in the play. She narrates certain incidents and conducts the play, while the Man and the Flames are used very much like the

Dolls of *Hayavadana*. The Flames, introduced in the prologue, play a vital role later in the play. The Prologue in *The Fire and the Rain* also provides background to the main action of the play. The devices of irony and supernatural elements are introduced in the prologue itself. It presents some of the main characters like Paravasu, Arvasu, Nittilai, the King, the actor-manager and his brother in the beginning. An important issue in the play—fire sacrifice versus theatre—comes under focus in the Prologue itself. Prologue and Epilogue put together form an independent plot that adds meaning to the rest of the play.

Karnad is aware of the importance of stage-lighting which has a style and character of its own. Light paints multiple pictures and ebbs and flows with the action of the drama. If *Hayavadana* is an innovative experiment in fusing together the traditional and the modern theatrical devices, *The Fire and the Rain* is a perfect fusion of music and light along with the use of mask. In the Prologue, after Paravasu permits the theatre troop to perform a play, we see Arvasu carrying a mask. The actor-manager and his limping brother are accompanied by a couple of women who are to provide music. The moment the actor-manager starts singing a benedictory verse, the stage darkens and only Arvasu is left in a "pool of light". The use of dimmers, gently fading the lights in or out, provides immense scope for magical possibilities in *Tughlaq*.

Elaborate stage directions for the use of modern stage devices like curtains, light and sound remain essential in the hands of the playwright. For instance, when Padmini performs sati in *Hayavadana*, stage directions for the curtain and song is are given:

> The stage-hands lift the curtain, slowly, very slowly, very slowly, as the song goes on. The curtain has a blazing fire painted on it. And as it is lifted, the flames seem to leap up. The female musicians sing a song. (*Three Plays* 131)

In the Shallow scenes in *Tale-Danda,* a painted curtain depicting a street as the backdrop is used, while the Deep scenes shows the interiors of palaces, the Brahmin's quarter, the Queen's chamber, the God's room, the inner chamber, the courtesan's quarters and the front yard of the palace. Apart from suggesting change of scene, the use of light enhances the over-all effect of action.

Music and exotic imagery create colourful improvisation. Each scene has a limited purpose with regard to the overall dramatic action. Sometimes Karnad uses chorus or song in order to suspend the flow of dramatic action and provide multiplicity of themes in *Tughlaq*. In *Hayavadana*, he has employed *Yakshagana* conventions like songs, music, *Bhagavata*, worship of Lord Ganesha at the opening, *Bhagavada Vakyam* at the end, stylized actions, etc. *Bhagavata*, accompanied by musicians, sings verses in praise of Lord Ganesha and narrates the story in the manner of a folk-tale. The female chorus, a folk device, gives expression to Padmini's longing and lust for Kapila. Karnad uses in the play poetry, music, a sense of gaiety and celebration traditionally associated with a theatrical event. In *Naga-Mandala*, the use of chorus and music are the notable features in which all the songs are sung by the Flames.

The action of the play in *Hayavadana* is mimed. For example, when Devadatta, Padmini and Kapila proceed to Ujjain, a cart does not appear on the stage, rather, Kapila followed by Padmini and Devadatta enter miming a card ride. Kapila is driving the cart (*Three Plays* 95). The play is replete with instances of miming.

Use of light, miming, freezing and quick shifts of scenes remains special features of *Naga-Mandala*. As the play starts, it is night and "Moonlight seeps in through cracks in the roof and in the walls" (22). On the moonlight stage Man and the flames are talking. In Act One the stage is lighted up to show that it is the daytime. But as Appanna leaves, Rani alone talking to herself, "her words become distinct as the lights dim" (27). Again, it is dark on the stage. The scene shifts into night and Rani is found dreaming of her parents. As she gets up, "it gets light" (28). She mimes splashing water on her eyes. Appanna also arrives and he mimes taking a bath in the bathroom. Taking bath is always staged through miming. The moment Appanna goes out, Rani falls asleep and the stage gets dark again. When Act II starts, it is again night as the Naga is seen caressing the sleeping Rani. Whenever Naga appears, it is dark as against Appanna who appears on the lighted upstage. Rani's disclosure of her pregnancy to Naga is followed by a sudden splash of light. They both freeze and the "lights change sharply from night to mid-day" (52). When Appanna goes to the village elders, the lights change into night again. Rani is found crying as Naga sits by her side on the floor. Again the stage is lighted up and the scene changes into the Village-Square. Use of lights makes the double role of Appanna possible. The same Appanna turns into Naga when the lights fade out. Music and light play an important role when Rani is declared a goddess. As the cobra slides up Rani's shoulders and moving over her shoulder spreads its hood on her head, "Music fills the skies. The lights change into a soft luminous glow" (58). The elders shout, "Palanquin! Music!" Later, Rani gently takes Appanna in her arms. Again there is music in the background as they speak to each other in an inaudible voice. Summoning his musical powers when Naga enters Rani's tresses, "beam of light is thrown on him" and "the rest is plunged into darkness" (62).

Karnad employs the ingenious folk device of masks which is a typical feature of *Yakshagana* to project the personalities of different characters. In the beginning of *Hayavadana*, a mask of Lord Ganesha is brought on the stage and kept on a chair for worship. Padmini's transposition of heads of Devadatta and Kapila is done through the use of masks. In *Fire and the Rain*, Arvasu wears the mask of demon Vritra.

The use of spectacles remains a special feature of Karnad's plays. It is done through scenery, lighting, costumes, make-ups and movement of the action. If father's youth and son's old age act as a major spectacle in Yayati, Appanna's double role in *Naga-Mandala* and mutual killing by Devadatta and Kapila and their coming back to life again in *Hayavadana*, the death scene of King Bijjala in *Tale-Danda* and the play-within-the-play in *Fire and the Rain* are produce spectacles on stage. The use of the supernatural is an inevitable feature in folk art. As folk art is meant to entertain the audience with limited intellect, the folk artist makes use of the supernatural to keep the audience absorbed. The presence of Goddess Kali in *Hayavadana*, Lord Indra in *Fire and the Rain*, and Naga in *Naga-Mandala* point to the folk element in Karnad's plays. Karnad hints that God's plans are different from men's. It is reflected in Vritra's (Arvasu's) words in *Fire and the Rain*: "They say gods should never be trusted.... Indeed, it's said that when the gods speak to us, the meaning they attach to each word is quite different from the meaning we humans attach to it. Thus their side of their speech often denies what our side of their speech promises (*Collected Plays*, Vol. 2, 168). This kind of portrayal of supernatural characters and the complex meanings they suggest makes Karnad's plays highly suggestive. Man's problems are his own. Gods cannot solve or give solution to human problems; it has to be devised by humans themselves.

Besides *Yakshagana* traditions, Karnad also follows company *natak* style. *Tughlaq* is written in the convention of the company *natak*. In a company *natak,* all the scenes are divided and alternated between deep scenes and shallow scenes. The shallow scene is usually a street scene and is meant for comedy. The shallow scene allows time for a change of sets for the deep scene. The shallow scene has comic characters, and crowds. It is like a comic sub-plot of a Shakespearean play. Witches in the first scene of *Macbeth*, Kent and Gloucester in *King Lear*, Marcellus, Horatio, and Barnardo and the ghost in *Hamlet*, Roderigo and the pernicious villain Iago in *Othello* and the Plebians in *Julius Caesar* appear and strike the keynote of the play. They appear in streets or deserted places. They play a dominant role in the play and finally the sub-plot merges with the main plot. In *Tughlaq*, the curtain open sin a palace. The characters of the play are clearly divided into two categories—the protagonist Tughlaq who dominate deep scenes and the minor characters like Aziz, Aazam and the crowd representing the Hindus and the Muslims which appear in shallow scenes. As the play advances, the comic characters of the shallow scenes merge with the main plot.

Animal imagery has always been widely used in folktales. Snakes have always been commanding an enviable position in folktales. The mystery associated with Cobra always commands a distinct place. It is important to note that King Cobra has been widely used for the delineation of complex themes and ideas in folk lores and legends. The legends knit around it further intensify the figurative implications inherent in it. The first spark of this complex image is realized when Kapanna compares Appanna with Cobra. When his mother was trying to console Rani in Appanna's absence, Kappanna says: "Mother, you can't do this! You can't start meddling in other people's affairs. The first thing in the morning. That Appanna should have been born a wild beast or a reptile. By some mistake, he got human birth. He can't understand other people. Why do you want to tangle with him" (*Three Plays* 28). It is interesting to note that the character of Kurudavva is a typical of folktale character, who contributes to the movement of the action in the play. She contrives to accelerate the action by subtle use of the supernatural women's role in folktales.

Karnad employs the tradition of oral narration in his plays. In *Hayavadana*, the Bhagavata narrates the story of Padmini, Kapila and Devadatta, befitting the manner of a folktale: "This is the city of Dharmapura, ruled by king Dharmasheela whose fame and empire have already reached the ends of the eight directions. Two youths who dwell in the city are our heroes. One is Devadatta..." (73). This oral structure of the narrative gives the play a distinctive indigenous style. Hayavadana's narration of his story is also in tune with the oral narrative form. Like a folktale, the play is a mixture of the human and non-humans, incomplete individuals, magnanimous gods, vocal dolls and mute children. Karnad uses all these to create a queer magical world. *Naga-Mandala* also follows an oral structure of narration. Act I begins with the Story narrating the tale of Rani perfectly like a folktale: "A young girl. Her name...it does not matter. But she was an only daughter, so her parents called her Rani. Queen..." (27).

Karnad employs the folk theatre techniques in his plays both as a weapon of resistance against the dominant colonial forms and as an effective tool for denaturalizing the realist modes of European theatre. He has applied the alienation effect of Brechtian theatre in the play through the innovative use of an indigenous Indian tradition. For example, he is closer to Brechtian anti-cathartic effect in his *Tughlaq*. When all his progressive measures fail, his good intentions fatally miscarry, when his amires conspire to kill him at prayer time for which he has to ban prayer, when his beloved subjects call him "Mad Mohammad! Mad Mohammad!" (196), when his step-mother assassinates his friend, Tughlaq cries:

> God, God in Heaven, please help me. Please don't let go of my hand. My skin drips with blood and I don't know how much of it is mine and how much of others. I started in Your path, Lord, why am I wandering naked in this desert flow? I started in search of You. Why am I become a pig rolling in this gory mud? Raise me. Clean me. Cover me with Your Infinite Mercy. I can only clutch at the hem of Your cloak with my bloody fingers and plead. I can only beg—have pity on me. I have no one but You now. Only You. Only You. You...You...You. (205-06)

His outburst of anguish sounds like King Lear's agonised cry:

> "Close pent-up guilts,
> Rive your concealing continents, and cry
> These dreadful summoners grace. I am a man
> More sinn'd against than sinning". (King Lear Act 3, Scene 2)

But Tughlaq's remorse lacks cathartic effect as the audience lack emotional identification with Tughlaq because he does not suffer from genuine repentance for all his wrong actions. No audience feels pity with Tughlaq. The playwright's motive to juxtapose the one scene where he is a benevolent king for Vishnu Sharma with another where he is so ruthless that he stabs even the dead body of Shihab-ud-din with a frenzy certainly incites the audience for the Brechtian 'complex seeing'—to see with a strange outlook the happenings on stage. His order to behead all the conspirators, stuff their bodies with straw and hang them up in the palace yard creates chaos in the minds of the audience/reader and does not arouse aesthetic pleasure. Thus, the audience would view the performance with a critical detachment—in Brecht's term *verfremdungseffekt* or 'alienation effect'—and judge the contemporary situation in the historical perspective for the better conditions of life. Similarly, the death of all three characters—Devadatta, Kapila and Padmini—in *Hayavadana* only shows the absurdity behind the situation leading to their death and does not strike a tragic note to create pity and fear in the audience necessary for a cathartic effect.

Influence of Brecht can be seen on Karnad in his use of songs. The purpose of song in his plays is not to heighten the emotion of the scenes but as a means to commentate or narrate what is going on. It is also a form of alienating the audience. This is evident in Brecht's *Mother Courage and Her Children*: the songs' content may be serious and forewarning of hardships, while the music is happy and light. It shows a lighter side to a deeply serious situation and the dichotomy and ambiguity of it ultimately alienates the audience and makes them question the social realities that are being presented. The music and the action should serve to make each other seem strange. Songs of the Flames in *Naga-Mandala* singing a chorus surrounding Naga and Rani as they sing and dance, Songs of Bhagavata and Padmini's lullaby in *Hayavadana* and the Queen and the King's songs in *Bali: The Sacrifice* have Brechtian alienation effect in the play.

The inculcation of pre-colonial past in the forms of indigenous performance like rituals, myths, folktales and history are effective devices in dismantling the dominating forms of Western dramaturgy. Karnad's employment of retrospective narratives of the myths, folktales and history of the nation can be seen as his strategy to bring in the elements of native culture to the dominant Eurocentric theatrical tradition.

WORKS CITED

Ansen, Kathrynh. "Indian Folk Traditions and the Modern Theatre", *Asian Folklore Studies,* Vol. 42, 1983.

Karnad, Girish. *Three Plays*. Delhi: OUP, 1994.

———. *Collected Plays*. Vol. 2. Delhi: OUP, 2005.

Mukherjee, Tutun. *Girish Karnad's Plays: Performance and Critical Perspectives*. Delhi: Pencraft International, 2006.

Paul, Rajinder. "Girish Karnad: An Interview by Kirtinath Kurtkoti," *Contemporary Indian Theatre: Interviews with Playwrights and Directors*. New Delhi: Sangeet Natak Akademi, 1989.

Shukla, Raj Rekha. "The Interweaving of Folk Strategies in the Plays of Karnad". Vol. III, 5-6 Jan-Dec, 2011. www.inflibnet.ac.in

ATLANTIC JOURNALS SUBSCRIPTION FORM

LIST OF OUR QUARTERLY JOURNALS

The Atlantic Critical Review	ISSN 0972-6373	English Literature	☐
The Atlantic Literary Review	ISSN 0972-3269	English Literature	☐
The Atlantic Review of Feminist Studies	ISSN 2320-5105	English Literature	☐

Tick (√) in box for the Journals you want to Subscribe

SUBSCRIPTION RATES FOR EACH JOURNAL

	SUBSCRIPTION PERIOD	SUBSCRIPTION RATES	
		INSTITUTIONAL	INDIVIDUAL
For SAARC COUNTRIES	Single Issue	₹ 750.00	₹ 600.00
	Annual (Four Issues)	₹ 2700.00	₹ 1500.00
	Two Years (Eight Issues)	₹ 5100.00	₹ 2700.00
	Back Issue (Per Issue)	₹ 750.00	₹ 600.00
For REST OF THE WORLD	Single Issue	US $ 105.00	US $ 75.00
	Annual (Four Issues)	US $ 300.00	US $ 90.00
	Two Years (Eight Issues)	US $ 525.00	US $ 150.00
	Back Issue (Per Issue)	US $ 105.00	US $ 75.00

Rupee rates apply to subscriptions from SAARC Countries only. Remittances from elsewhere should be in US dollars or its equivalent in Pound, Euro or Indian Rupees. Subscriptions should be sent through Demand Draft/Cheque payable at New Delhi in favour of **'Atlantic Publishers and Distributors (P) Ltd.'** Outstation cheques should include ₹ 40.00 in India and US $ 10.00 abroad towards bank collection charges.

For Direct Bank Transfer, refer details as below:

Account Name: Atlantic Publishers and Distributors (P) Ltd.
Account No.: 0333 0500 1505, IFSC: ICIC0000333
Bank, Branch: ICICI Bank, Ansari Road, Darya Ganj
After transfer, please intimate by sending an email to editorial@atlanticbooks.com or phone: 011-40775300.

YES! I/We wish to Subscribe ☐ **Renew** ☐ **(Please use Block Letters)**

Name: Mr./Mrs./Ms. ____________________ Designation ____________________

Organisation: ____

Address: ____

City: ______________ State: ______________ Pin: ______________

Tel. Off. ______________ Resi: ______________ Mobile: ______________ Email: ______________
with STD code with STD code

Subscription starting from: Quarter: ______________ Year: ______________

Details in case of Back Issue: ____

Enclosed is a Cheque No. ________ DD No. ________ Bank Transfer ________ Date ________
made payable at New Delhi favouring **Atlantic Publishers and Distributors (P) Ltd.**

Date: ______________ Signature of Subscriber ______________

Please fill and mail this subscription form along with DD/Cheque/Bank Transfer Details to

The Subscription Division
ATLANTIC PUBLISHERS AND DISTRIBUTORS (P) LTD.
B-2, Vishal Enclave, Opp. Rajouri Garden, New Delhi-110 027, India
Tel: 011-40775300, 40775301, 25413460, 25429987 • email: editorial@atlanticbooks.com